John Bates Clark

The Philosophy of Wealth

Economic Principles Newly Formulated

John Bates Clark

The Philosophy of Wealth
Economic Principles Newly Formulated

ISBN/EAN: 9783337073558

Printed in Europe, USA, Canada, Australia, Japan

Cover: Foto ©Suzi / pixelio.de

More available books at **www.hansebooks.com**

THE PHILOSOPHY OF WEALTH

Also Published In

REPRINTS OF ECONOMIC CLASSICS

By John Bates Clark

THE DISTRIBUTION OF WEALTH [1899]

THE

PHILOSOPHY OF WEALTH

ECONOMIC PRINCIPLES NEWLY FORMULATED

BY

JOHN BATES CLARK

[1886]

REPRINTS OF ECONOMIC CLASSICS

Augustus M. Kelley Publishers
New York   1967

First Edition 1886

(Boston: Ginn & Co., *Publishers*, 1886)

Second Edition 1887

Reprinted 1967 by

AUGUSTUS M. KELLEY PUBLISHERS

Library of Congress Catalogue Card Number

67-25955

PRINTED IN THE UNITED STATES OF AMERICA
by SENTRY PRESS, NEW YORK, N. Y. 10019

THE

PHILOSOPHY OF WEALTH.

ECONOMIC PRINCIPLES NEWLY FORMULATED.

BY

JOHN B. CLARK, A.M.,

PROFESSOR OF HISTORY AND POLITICAL SCIENCE IN SMITH COLLEGE.

———————

BOSTON, U.S.A.:

GINN & COMPANY, PUBLISHERS.

1887

PREFACE.

In a series of articles in the *New Englander*, commenced ten years ago, I endeavored to contribute a share toward the reformulating of certain leading principles of economic science. The traditional system was obviously defective in its premises. These were assumptions rather than facts, and the conclusions deduced from them were, for that reason, uncertain. The assumed premises were, at certain points, at variance with facts, and the conclusions were, to that extent, erroneous. The better elements of human nature were a forgotten factor in certain economic calculations; the man of the scientific formula was more mechanical and more selfish than the man of the actual world. A degraded conception of human nature vitiated the theory of the distribution of wealth.

The prevalent theory of value started with a misconception of utility, and of the part which it plays in exchanges. Economic science, in general, found no adequate place for the intellectual activities of men, and made no important use of the fact that society is an organism, to be treated as a unit in the discussion of many processes affecting wealth.

The articles referred to endeavored to contribute such share as they might toward the needed reconstruction of economic theories. They endeavored to broaden the conception of wealth, as the subject of the science, to find a place in the system for the better motives of human nature, to construct a new theory of value, to apply at all points the organic conception of society, and to suggest other corrections. They tried, in general, to bring the premises of the science into better accordance with facts, and to bring the general spirit of it into greater harmony with the instinctive demands of a healthy human nature.

In this book the most of these articles are republished, with varying amounts of revision, and the discussion is extended, and made to include, among other points, a study of the nature of production and distribution. The one process is found to consist of a synthesis, and the other of an analysis; the same elements which are combined in production are separated, step by step, in distribution. The process loosely termed competition is analyzed, and a new theory of "non-competing groups" is advanced, and applied to the labor problem. The lines furnished by these groups are found to determine the limits of the combinations of capital and of labor, which are the distinctive feature of the present era. A study is made of the laws determining what forms of industrial organization shall emerge from the present chaotic condition. The test of economic principles is applied to the intellectual and spiritual activities of society.

There are two or three points in the system, as here outlined, which readers of recent economic literature might naturally suppose were directly borrowed from that source. These were, however, contained in the articles already referred to, which were published early enough to preclude dependence on anything very recently issued. Whatever may be their merits or demerits, the theories here advanced are not borrowed from the writings of other persons.

If this book were intended as a general treatise on political economy, it would, of course, be very incomplete. It omits whatever belongs to that field which is common to economics and practical politics. It has nothing to say about protection or currency. Obviously the work cannot be a text-book, in the ordinary sense of the term. Teachers who do not want a text-book as the sole or chief means of instruction, and who prefer to present in their own way the controverted practical questions of the day, may, perhaps, find a place for it in the classroom. The place which it primarily seeks is in the hands of readers and thinkers who have long been in revolt against the general spirit of the old political economy.

J. B. CLARK.

PREFACE TO THE SECOND EDITION.

I COMPLY with the suggestion of a friendly critic in stating the relation which the theory of value advanced in the fifth chapter of this book bears to that of Professor Jevons. My theory was attained independently, very long ago, but proved to coincide with that of Professor Jevons in the general fact of establishing a close connection between utility and value in exchange, and in regarding utility as subject to mental measurements. In some more specific points it resembled that theory without quite coinciding with it. It has been published without change in any of these respects. Features of the theory which I still venture to regard as my own are the identification of value in all its forms with measure of utility, the distinction between absolute and effective utility, and the analysis of the part played by society as an organic whole in the valuing processes of the market.

Of the twelve chapters of the book, nine treat of topics falling within the traditional limits of economic science; while the remaining three discuss subjects which a highly orthodox view may perhaps regard as lying outside of economic limits. If, however, political economy undertakes to discuss wealth in all its forms, and to analyze the forces which actually influence the distribution of it, it is difficult to see how these topics can be excluded from the discussion. Those who believe in a progressive system of economic science will probably not desire to exclude them.

J. B. CLARK.

NORTHAMPTON, MASS.,
FEB. 2, 1887.

CONTENTS.

CHAPTER IX.

CHAPTER I.

WEALTH.

PRACTICAL wisdom was never more in demand than at present. Questions concerning currency, free-trade, transportation, etc., are demanding and receiving the attention of political economists, and it is in this part of their science that the attractive fields lie both for the writer and the reader. The period of irreconcilable diversity in the fundamental principles of the science seems to be past, and one of relative unanimity, in thought if not in language, appears to have arrived. May theoretical work, then, be laid definitely aside? Not unless fundamental truths are of less importance here than in other departments of human thinking, and not unless the unanimity concerning them is something more than relative. If obscurity still hangs over principles, the clear apprehension of which is essential to all reasoning on the subject, the removal of it, besides having an incalculable value in itself, will afford a welcome supplement to directly practical work. It will shed light on the pressing social questions of the day. In the present state of the public mind, for example, financial heresies and strange teachings concerning the rights of property find a ready circulation; and, if these false doctrines connect themselves, even remotely, with fundamental errors of political economy, then the assault upon the practical fallacies can never be quite successful until the underlying errors be exposed and corrected. Questions on the solution of which the general prosperity depends cannot be solved without the clear apprehension of correct principles.

Nothing can be more fundamental in economic science than the conception of wealth. Is it worth our while to take issue with the current definitions of it? Not if the question to be settled is one of terms merely, and if the underlying thought is clear. Exactly the reverse of this is true of the definition of wealth which John Stuart Mill has inherited from Adam Smith, and, in turn, bequeathed to the so-called orthodox school of political economy. The terms of this definition are not seriously objectionable, but the thought which, in the discussion, they have been made to convey is so inconsistent with the significance of the terms themselves as to carry confusion throughout the science.

Mr. Mill's conception of wealth is so limited as to exclude much that is obviously a proper subject of economic study. It has obliged him to revive the pernicious classification of labor as productive and unproductive, and expressly to exclude from the list of productive laborers such persons as "the actor, the musical performer, the public declaimer or reciter, and the showman "; also "the army and navy, the legislator, the judge, and the officer of justice." On the other hand, certain economists under the leadership of M. Bastiat, impressed by the evils resulting from the traditional classification, have found no other remedy than that of abandoning the conception, wealth, as the subject of their science.

Yet there is a certain definable thing which is and must be the subject of political economy. Whether avowed or not, a definite conception is, in reality, under discussion in every treatise on this science. For this conception the term wealth, if used in the strictest accordance with history and etymology, is an accurate designation. The Saxon *weal* indicated a condition of relative well-being, the state of having one's wants well supplied as compared with a prevailing standard. No possession common to all men can constitute such relative well-being. The limitless gifts of nature do not produce it, since they are indiscriminating in their ministrations; air and sunlight make no differences among men, and, though creating absolute well-being, cannot create that social condition indicated by the term wealth. This relative condition can be produced only by that which, besides satisfying wants, is capable of appropriation.

It is by a transfer of meaning that the term which primarily designated a condition of life has been applied to the things which produce the condition. But not all causes of comparative happiness are included in the meaning of the word. Wealth, as historically used, signified the well-being resulting from outward rather than inward causes. Health and contentment may make the shepherd happier than the owner of flocks; yet the owner only is "well off." Reserving a broader term to designate well-being in general, usage has employed the word wealth to signify, first, the comparative welfare resulting from material possessions, and secondly, and by a transfer, the possessions themselves.

Wealth then consists in the relative-weal-constituting elements in man's material environment. It is objective to the user, material, useful, and appropriable. Let us apply the term with logical consistency to whatever possesses these four essential attributes, and note the effect on the traditional conception of wealth. Mr. Mill and the orthodox school will be found to exclude from their classification things which possess these attributes, and to include some which do not. They recognize as wealth only those things which are sufficiently substantial and durable to constitute a more or less permanent possession, things which would appear on the inventory, if society were suddenly to cease producing and consuming, and apply itself, for, say, a month or two, to taking an account of stock. It is here maintained that durability is not an essential attribute of wealth. Durability is a factor of *value*, and determines, in so far, the measure of wealth in any particular product. But products are of all degrees of durability, and there is no ground for excluding any of them from the conception of wealth on the ground of this simple difference of degree. Even the school of writers referred to would not hesitate to class the ices of the confectioner in the same category with the stone wall of the mason, though they are at opposite extremes in the scale of durability. They would, however, exclude music from the conception, on the ground of its insubstantial and perishable character. It is maintained in this discussion that, in that which constitutes wealth, there is no difference other than one of degree between music and a stone wall. The difference in their durability is, indeed, one of the factors in their relative value ; but both alike possess the four essential attributes above specified ; they are objective and material products ; they are useful and appropriable, and fall within the definition of wealth.

Having unduly limited their conception of wealth in one direction, the orthodox writers have unduly extended it in another. They have, for example, classed as wealth the acquired skill and the technical knowledge of the laborer. Personal attainments, as subjective and immaterial, are excluded from the meaning of the term. They are not a possession ; that implies externality to the possessor. They are what he is, not what he has. Popular thought and speech broadly dis-

tinguish the able man from the wealthy man. A man
has a potential fortune, not an actual one, in his abilities. The term indicates a state of being able, and
implies a possibility; not an attained result. Labor
creates wealth, and acquired abilities are potential
labor. They are to be regarded as the potentiality of
the human factor of production, and it introduces an
element of confusion into the science to class them with
the completed product. If these considerations were
not sufficient to settle the economic status of a man's
subjective qualities, it would, at least, suffice for that
end to apply to them the test of the traditional definition itself, in which "exchangeable value" is made to
be the essential attribute of wealth. In every exchange
two commodities are alienated, and transferred to new
ownership. Nothing can be subjected to this process
which is an inseparable part of one man's being.

The error of putting abilities and products in the
same category is wide-spread, and appears in the writings of some of Mr. Mill's opponents. As acute a thinker
as J. B. Say characterizes acquired talents as "a species
of wealth, notwithstanding its immateriality, so little imaginary that, in the shape of professional services, it is
daily exchanged for gold and silver." The illustration
is its own best answer. The talents are not alienated,
and cannot be so; the lawyer does not deprive himself
of them, nor does his client acquire them, by the rendering of legal service. Their product only is trans-

ferable, and that only is a commodity. It will hereafter
be shown that the human effort which creates a product
calls into exercise activities physical, mental and moral.
If wealth-creating abilities are to be confounded with
the product which results from exercising them, every
power acquired by effort, involving, in practice, the
whole man, will have to be classed as a commodity.
The error is mentally confusing, and it is disastrous in
its practical results. Man produces wealth and consumes it; but man himself is always distinct from it.

The illustration just cited suggests an examination of
the "service" theory of M. Bastiat. As alchemists,
searching unsuccessfully for gold, discovered com-
pounds from which oxygen might be extracted, so
those who have sought for a substitute for wealth, as a
fundamental conception of economic science, have attained a compound notion the analysis of which gives
something which is to the economic theory what oxygen
is to the chemical.

According to M. Bastiat it is services only that are
exchanged in the market: commodities, indeed, pass
from hand to hand; but they are services materialized,
while others remain without material embodiment.
"Do this for me, and I will do that for you," is the formula for the exchange of services in their immaterial
state; "give me what you have done, and I will give
you what I have done" is the formula for the exchange
of commodities.

Now a service consists of an effort and a gratification. In order that it may exist, some one must labor,
and some one's want must be satisfied. It is apparent
that effort, as such, gratifies no one. An artisan's
effort gives pleasure only through the medium of the
commodity which he produces. The efforts of a body-
servant give satisfaction only through the modifications
which they effect in the master's environment; and
apart from this they would certainly not be wanted.
Effort is irksome to the laborer, and, by the law of sympathy, it is irksome to those who witness it; without
outward results, it would be intolerable to an employer. A musician's effort is displeasing in itself,
though the annoyance which the display of it occasions is counterbalanced, and a large balance of
enjoyment is secured, by the objective effect, — musical sound. This principle may be easily tested. Let an
accomplished pianist advertise a concert on one of Mr.
Petersilea's mute piano-fortes, and promise to display
a large amount of effort; how many tickets, at a dollar
each, would he probably sell? Let a voiceless speaker
attempt to entertain an audience by a similar display of
effort; how long would the assembly remain together?
Yet, in either case, absolutely nothing would be wanting but the tenuous outward product, — sound.

The objective element inseparable from service is
wealth; the totality of it is the sum total of social
products. This material element is the result of effort

and the cause of gratification, and furnishes, therefore, the necessary connection between the elements of service. It has invariably the four essential attributes of wealth; it is objective to the producer and the utilizer; it is material, useful and appropriable. It is distinguishable in every action that can be termed a service; but it is not always tangible, visible and durable. It is a mark of progressing civilization when the products of labor, the objective elements in service, take as their basis the more tenuous materials given in nature. It marks a certain supremacy over natural forces when man hews stone and fashions timber; it marks an intellectual sovereignty when the thought of man impresses itself on vibrating air or makes electricity its messenger to remote regions. It is the more ethereal products of human effort that are the characteristic wealth of a highly organized society.

CHAPTER II.

LABOR AND ITS RELATION TO WEALTH.

LABOR is the former of the two subjective elements in service, namely, the wealth-creating effort. It is the making nature subservient to a master, and the primitive mode of doing this is by simply determining what master an already useful element shall serve.

Relative weal results from the mere appropriation of limited natural gifts. With the unlimited gifts monopoly is impossible; the ultra-democracy of air and sunlight insist on creating, in so far as their ministrations can do it, a weal that is equal and universal. But primitive man may pluck the wild fruit or slay the game in his natural Eden, and then vindicate by effort his right to enjoy them. He may select a dwelling-place, proclaim it his own, and repel intruders; he may guard the fruit-yielding tree, and even the hunting ground itself. This is almost the only form of labor which exists in the most primitive social state. Man, here, lives by the mere appropriation of the spontaneous products of tropical nature, and expends his chief efforts in guarding his property. The capacity to be thus owned and utilized is a primary attribute of wealth.

The condition of appropriation is a relation between commodities, on the one hand, and persons, on the other, and implies, therefore, that both the commodity itself and the society where it exists should be such that the relation may be established. The commodity must exist in limited quantity, and must be of a nature capable of being retained in the possession of a particular user. The atmosphere, as a whole, is inappropriable from its unlimited quantity; while pleasing atmospheric effects, cloud scenery, showers or breezes are limited in quantity, but are inappropriable from their nature. They minister transiently to whomsoever they will, and, in the long run, with impartiality. Except as rain-drops mingle with the earth, or as breezes and sunset-colors favor the dwellers in an elevated locality, and thus impart a value to the land itself, there is no power in man to determine the direction of their ministrations. The ownership of land carries with it only a partial control of the benefits of these elusive elements in nature. Utilities which are, from their nature, inappropriable constitute an important and neglected subject of economic study.

On the part of the society where the commodity exists something is also requisite, in order that the relation of ownership may subsist. The attributes of society which render ownership possible are, it is believed, usually ignored altogether in treatises on this subject. The existence of these attributes is secured

by the labor of a distinct class of persons, whose true
economic function cannot be apprehended without
noticing the effect of their labors upon society, and
thus, indirectly, upon the wealth which exists in
society.

In order that the essential attribute of wealth, appropriability, may be realized, the rights of property
must be recognized and enforced, either by personal
prowess, or by the agency of legal functionaries. In
the most primitive of societies the guarding of property
is done by each owner for himself, and constitutes, as
above stated, his only regular labor. The earliest general division of labor consists in assigning the protec-
tive function to men, uniting with it the congenial work
of hunting wild game, and reserving the more onerous
industrial functions for women. Civilization partially
reverses this arrangement; it includes the majority of
men in the industrial ranks, and excludes women from
the heaviest tasks; but it still reserves a limited class
of men for the work of protecting property. Comparatively few officers of justice render property so secure that whatever a man produces becomes his in
the act of production, and remains in his possession,
with but a minimum of thought and effort on his own
part. Useful things are now appropriable in so far
as the condition of society is concerned.

In the securing of this result the definition of rights
is as important as their enforcement, and legislators

and judges, as well as sheriffs, are, therefore, instrumental in producing that social condition which is necessary in order that the attribute of wealth, appropriability, may be realized. Whoever makes, interprets, or enforces law produces wealth. He imparts to the commodities of the society which employs him the essential wealth-constituting attribute of appropriability. Commodities may exist in society, and may possess any degree of utility; they may even be appropriable, as far as they are themselves concerned; but if social causes prevent their attaining the state of appropriation, they lack, in fact, the attribute of appropriability, and are not actual wealth. The production of social modifications which result in giving to commodities the attribute of appropriability is the chief economic function of legislative and judicial labor. It is as truly a wealth-creating function as the direct production of useful commodities.

Concerning this important class of laborers much misconception has existed. Mr. Mill, repeating the error of Adam Smith, classes them as unproductive. M. Bastiat, M. Garnier and others term their efforts "services," but offer no satisfactory substantive conception of anything as a product of their labor. Mr. J. B. Say, one degree nearer to the truth, classes them as producers, on the ground that they enable the industrial classes to give their undivided efforts to their own occupation, and thus contribute indirectly to their

products. This indirect mode of proving that a class
of laborers is productive, though plausible and frequently employed, is extremely objectionable. Every
class of producers contributes in this manner to the
products of every other. The shoemaker contributes
indirectly to the productions of the farmer, by saving
him the necessity of turning aside from his labor to
mend shoes; yet he considers that the shoes, and not
a share in the farmer's harvest, are the direct product
of his labor. In like manner the farmer contributes
indirectly to the productions of the shoemaker, by
saving him the necessity of turning aside from his occupation to cultivate the ground; yet the farmer re-
gards his grain, and not a share in the shoes, as the
product of his labor. A direct product must be exchanged if any class of producers is to share in the
wealth created by another, and every class must have
a direct product if they are to be classed as productive laborers. The direct product which legal officers
offer in return for their support consists in the attribute of appropriability which they impart to commodities. They put, as it were, the finishing touch to
the products of society, which finishing touch renders
them marketable wealth; and this modification, which
constitutes a difference between potential and actual
wealth, is that which they exchange for their subsistence. If the term productive were to be taken in a
narrow sense, as meaning productive, not of wealth,

but of specific useful commodities, there would be
ground for classing these laborers as unproductive;
and this is the origin of the misapprehension concerning them that has existed from the time of Adam
Smith to the present day. These classes are protec-
tive of useful commodities, but are productive of
wealth.

All forms of labor create wealth;* yet for every
product nature furnishes the substance and man only
the modes. One class of laborers create, as has been
shown, the attribute of appropriability; the other
general class create the attribute of utility. The latter is invariably accomplished by producing modifications in natural agents objective to the laborer. Industrial labor is always the applying of a human
effort to a natural agent. The modification produced
enables the agent to satisfy a want which it was
previously incapable of satisfying. This want-satisfying power imparted by labor is a "utility," and,
if the attribute of appropriability be also conferred,
wealth is created. A natural agent possessing utility
and appropriability is wealth, and this only is so.
The natural agent need not be of a substantial or
permanent character; any substance, force or activity
whatsoever in physical nature, which receives a want-
satisfying power by means of a laborer's efforts,
appropriability being presupposed, becomes wealth;
and, though its duration be but momentary, and its

* Particular cases of wasted effort are not here considered.

character insubstantial or intangible, there is no
ground for excluding it from the category so long as
its brief utility continues.

Dr. Roscher has called attention to the intrinsic
absurdity of calling a violin manufacturer a productive laborer, and the artist who plays the violin an
unproductive one, as is expressly done by Mr. Mill
and his followers. The violin would, thus, be classed
as wealth; the music, the sole end of its manufacture,
not wealth. The product, music, satisfies a direct
want, the violin only an indirect one; the latter is
an instrument for producing that which satisfies direct
desire. The direct want-satisfying product is, if anything, more obviously wealth than the indirect one.
Relative durability and tangibility are non-essential
attributes. The mechanic who makes the violin imparts utility to wood; the artist who plays it imparts
utility to air vibrations. One product is perceived
by the senses of sight and touch, the other by the
sense of hearing. One is extremely durable, the
other extremely perishable; but both alike come under our definition. In both a natural agent has received a utility through human effort; both products
are wealth, and both laborers productive.

So the sculptor imparts utility to marble, the painter
to colors, the photographer to chemical agencies and
solar light. The designer and the mechanical draughts-
man impart a high utility to a small amount of plum-

bago, and the writer to a small amount of ink. No
utility of a higher order is conceivable than that
which the writer imparts to ink and paper, and the
speaker to vibrating air, namely, the capacity for
conveying intelligence. A bridge across a stream
renders an interchange of products possible between
dwellers on opposite banks. Previously each side
produced for itself; after the building of the bridge
they produce partly for each other, and to the great
advantage of both. Two isolated societies become, by
virtue of the interactivity caused by the bridge, one
organism. Publications are mind-bridges; they render an interchange of mental products possible, as
the bridge over the stream does of material products. Mental interactivities take place by means
of the mind-bridge, as physical ones do by the ordinary bridge. Minds are united in organic life by the
one means of communication, as bodily activities are
by the other. If the writings of an author are a
mind-bridge, the words of a speaker are a mind-ferry.
As the ferry-boat conveys a farmer's produce to the
market, so the words of a public speaker, floating on
air, as a boat on water, convey his intellectual products
to the place where they find their market. The
mason imparts utility to the stone of the bridge, and
the boat-builder to the wood of the boat; the writer
imparts a higher utility to ink, and the speaker to
sound. All are productive laborers; their products,

in each case, are utilities imparted to natural agents, and fall within our definition of wealth. But it is the intellectual fashioners of tenuous material who are social workers *par excellence*, since the diffusion of thought which their products ensure gives intellectual life to the social organism.

It is obvious that, in literary and oratorical products, the utility imparted by the human effort vastly transcends the natural agent which is its substantial basis. The articulate sounds of the speaker are the ferry-boat; the ideas are the cargo, and the latter may exceed the former in value to an indefinite extent. In this case boat and cargo are a simultaneous product; the boat is fitted, in form, to every different lading, and the two, as an industrial product, are inseparable. This illustration affords the most searching test of our definition of wealth. The thought, as existing in the mind of the speaker previous to its utterance in words, does not fall within the conception. It is subjective to the man, and, like his mental faculty itself, is inalienable. It only acquires the attribute of transferability when it attaches itself to the agent, — the vocal sound. This apparently trifling agent transforms it from a simple activity into an industrial product. Again, with the consumers, the audience, the thought continues to exist, or, at least, other thought induced by it does so; but, after parting with its material vehicle, the sounds that convey it, it loses the attribute of transferability, and becomes again a simple activity, not an industrial product. To again become an industrial product, it must be freighted again on vocal sounds. Then only can it be transferred from hand to hand, receive its price in the market, and, for the brief period of its duration, be entitled to its place on the inventory of social wealth.

As the widest range of application is given to the term natural agent, so an equally broad application must be given to the term labor. The human activity which produces wealth is an activity of the entire man, physical, mental and moral, and there is no industrial product so simple and so purely material that these three elements of the human agency are not represented in it. In proportion as the intellectual element in the labor predominates over the physical, and as the moral element predominates over both, the product rises in the scale of respectability and of value. The labor of a stone-mason involves a physical effort in the simple moving of materials, an intellectual effort in their skilful combination, and a moral effort in the conscientious use of proper materials and methods. The result of the physical effort is seen in the position of the materials that have been moved in the construction, that of the intellectual effort in their strong and tasteful arrangement, and that of the moral effort in the certainty that, in ways not obvious to the eye, the inter-

ests of the owner have been consulted by the builder,
at his own expense, and that the wall is, in all respects,
as strong and as durable as it seems. In literary, professional, and educational labor, the intellectual element,
of course, predominates to an indefinite extent over the
physical, and the moral element is greatly increased.
The latter appears, in the labor of the writer, in his
sincerity of purpose; in that of the lawyer and the phy-
sician, in their disinterestedness; and, in all the more
intellectual kinds of labor, in their general faithfulness
and conscientiousness. Reliability is an attribute of
the product in each case, and the moral factor in the
labor is that which produces it.

The debated question whether moral qualities are
paid for is thus simply and easily decided. The
product is paid for; reliability is an attribute of the
product which determines its value, and the laborer
who can produce something having the attribute of
reliability can secure an enhanced price for it in the
market. All labor is indirectly paid for; its com-
pensation is in the market value of its product,
and, in so far as moral efforts are represented in an
industrial product, they are paid for as truly as other
activities of the laborer. No activities of man, physical,
mental, or moral, are paid for when not embodied in an
industrial product, and it is of importance to remember
that labor, as such, is not paid for. No employer takes
pleasure in the sweat of his laborer's brow; he regrets

it, and would willingly pay the same compensation to the same person if that particular product could be produced, by that person only, without effort. The product is the desired object in each case, and the labor, apart from its product, is not paid for and is never a commodity, and nothing but confusion results from so viewing and treating it. The statement so frequently met with in works on Political Economy that "labor is a commodity and is governed by the same laws as other commodities" is one of the mischievous errors that still cling to the science. The law of wages, the subject of desperate controversy, is, as we shall soon see, placed in a new and clear light when one apprehends, in its full bearing, the principle that the wage of labor is the market value of its product.

In view of the constant presence of these three elements in labor, the physical, the mental, and the moral, any effort, in the supposed interest of the working classes, to depreciate mental labor in comparison with physical is unintelligent. All labor is mental. To a large and controlling extent the mental element is present in the simplest operations. With the laborer who shovels in the gravel pit the directing and controlling influence of the mind predominates, to an indefinite extent, over the simple foot-pounds of mechanical force which he exerts. The latter could be better furnished by an ox. It would take certainly three stout men to exert as many foot-pounds of force as a single

ox, and if such a laborer is able to secure larger wages
than the third part of the cost of the labor of an ox, he
may place the difference to the credit of intellectual
labor. The numerical estimate has been made liberal,
since something is to be allowed for the superior physical form of the man.

Whatever possesses want-satisfying capacity and
appropriability is a form of wealth, whatever may be
the source from which it comes. Its origin is unimpor-
tant in the classification, and it may or may not be the
result of human labor. In some instances it is not so.
The original and indestructible properties of the soil
are not the result of human effort, and recent German
thought has demonstrated that they possess an original
value, from limitation in quantity, independently of the
increased value which results from their artificial improvement. The original forest trees, water powers,
minerals, some wild game, and many other things owe
the value which they possess to their want-satisfying
capacity, and their appropriability, not to the mode of
their origin. That origin is not labor. The *measure
of their value* is determined, in an indirect and general
manner, by labor. A man might be willing to give for
one of these spontaneous products of nature the amount
of labor which would produce or purchase another
product of equal utility. Labor is the measurer, not
the originator, of their utility, and even as a measurer
is indirect and tardy in its operation. The doctrine

that labor is the sole originator of wealth is, perhaps, the central doctrine in the system of Adam Smith, and it was an efficient instrument in his hands for combating the Mercantilists and the Physiocrats. It was accepted as a grand truth, as opposed to these pernicious systems, and it has served the purpose of a truth in the history of the science. It is, in fact, a grand error, and the time has abundantly arrived for its critical examination and essential modification.

Few statements are more common in text-books of Political Economy than the assertion that "nothing can constitute wealth which is not the product of labor." As the statement stands it can only mean that every commodity classed as wealth must have actually been produced by labor. In this form it requires but a single illustration to refute it. The original and indestructible properties of land are wealth, and they are not the product of labor. It is less erroneous to say that, though commodities may be produced by nature, their exchange value is the product of labor. A diamond accidentally discovered does not owe its utility to any labor actually expended in its production; but it does owe the measure of its value to a calculation in the mind of the purchaser as to how much labor would be necessary in order to obtain another like it. The seller will demand and the buyer will give what would purchase a similar commodity. Actual labor is not the criterion, but supposed labor, or mental considerations relative to labor. Utility is here given in nature without labor; value is measured by a calculation in which supposed labor is a basis. It is only when questions of quantity are considered and the measure of this value determined, that even considerations of labor are introduced. The measure of the exchange value of all commodities is determined indirectly, approximately and tardily, by considerations relative to labor. So much only of this doctrine can be maintained. A few simple illustrations will sufficiently establish this point. Suppose a chance medical discovery were to create a demand for some plant previously valueless. The plant would have value immediately, and would at once be exchangeable for something; but, ignoring the additional value resulting from gathering it, its value in the field would not be traceable to any labor expended in its production. For a time it would be unknown how much labor would be necessary for its production, and during this time, neither the fact of its utility nor the measure of its value could be referred to considerations of labor. Only after a time would labor determine this measure. If labor were a talisman which turned everything to gold, the slag of a blast-furnace should have value as well as the iron. The difference between them is in their utility, not in their origin. A chance chemical discovery might reveal uses for the slags in their present form, and they would then become wealth; but they would have been a product of labor before they became wealth as well as after. The existence of their newly-acquired utility could not be referred to labor, and for a time even their value could not be so determined. Aside from questions of measure, wealth is directly traceable, not to labor, but to the want-satisfying capacity and the appropriability of commodities.

Not every form of wealth is created by labor; but every form of labor creates wealth. Man toils, not because labor always precedes wealth, but because wealth naturally follows labor. The possession of want-satisfying products is what the laborer seeks, and desire is the moving force in the whole process. Labor is not to be conceived of as the *vis a tergo* that pushes wealth forward; but wealth is to be conceived of as the siren that lures labor onward. Wealth is always the cause of labor; labor is not always the cause of wealth. There are spontaneous natural products, and there are industrial products; the earth may be self-subdued, or it may be subdued by labor. Nature subjected and appropriated is wealth; man's subjection of nature is labor.

Labor imparts want-satisfying powers, or utilities, to natural agents. These utilities are of four kinds, and may be arranged in four corresponding classes, namely, elementary utility, form utility, place utility and time utility. New matter can not be created by man; but by chemical and vital changes in existing matter new material may be produced. The production of new material creates elementary utility, and this is preëminently the province of the agriculturist. Mining involves some change of place in the ore, but the labor of discovering and freeing it from the superincumbent earth is, prominently, a creating of elementary value, and mining should, in general, be classed with agriculture.

Existing materials generally require changes of form to fit them for satisfying wants, and the quality imparted by these changes is form utility. This is the office of the manufacturer, and, to a large extent, of the merchant. The forming of wool into cloth, of iron into tools, of wood into buildings, of stone into walls, etc., are obvious illustrations. The subdivision of articles purchased in bulk to suit the wants of the consumer is to be regarded as the creation of form utility. The man who desires only a pound of a particular commodity can afford to pay for it at a higher rate than if he were compelled to purchase a supply greatly in excess of his needs. The adaptation of the quantity to his needs creates an actual utility for him, and brings many enjoyments within his reach which would be otherwise unattainable. Subdivision creates form value, and its reward is legitimate.

A material in the requisite form may need removal

to the proper place in order to enable it to satisfy wants. Transportation confers on commodities the utility of being where they are wanted, and creates place utility. This is obviously created when commodities are brought to the consumer, but is not less truly created when the consumer is carried to the commodity. Place utility lies in the relative position of consumer and commodity, and both freight and passenger traffic produce it. The fact that it is relative and not absolute place which determines this utility distinguishes it from form value, as in manufactures. Manufacturing processes can be resolved, in the last analysis, into changes of place. The carpenter moves shavings and chips from the wood which he is shaping. The mason locates brick and mortar in contact with one another. The woolen manufacturer locates fibres of wool and coloring matter in certain positions. All these changes of place are irrespective of the consumer, and result only in giving form to the product, while place utility requires a relative position of the consumer and commodity.

A material in the necessary form and place may not be so at the requisite time for satisfying wants. Ice in winter, agricultural implements out of season, and, in general, all commodities at a time when they are not wanted, are obvious illustrations of products requiring this additional utility to fit them for consumption. The fact of existing at a time when

it is wanted gives to a commodity the attribute of time
utility. The creation of this value is the office of
capital, and the nature of capital does not come within
the limits of this discussion; but it is sufficiently
obvious that time value results from human effort and
abstinence. Its creation is a chief function of the
merchant, and it is of inestimable benefit to his customers. If every consumer were obliged to keep on
hand a supply of what he requires for sustenance and
comfort during indefinite periods of disuse, the number
of comforts which individuals could enjoy would be
reduced to a minimum. The idle capital of society
would be increased a hundred-fold and the list of
its comforts proportionately reduced. The creation of
time utility by the merchant is one of the most beneficent of human industries, and its reward one of the
most legitimate.

Having defined our conception of Wealth, Labor
and Utility, it may be well to apply to the definition a
few of the cases most difficult of classification under
prevailing systems. All artistic productions are crea-
tions of form utility, and differ from each other only
in the different agents to which this quality is imparted; the architect imparts it to buildings, the sculptor to marble, the painter to colors. The musician
imparts it to the natural agent, sound, and the public
reciter and speaker give a different kind of form value
to the same natural agent. The teacher is a pro-

ducer of form and place value, more especially of the latter. The confusion which arises from considering that the product of the teacher's labor is found in the mind of the pupil has already been noticed. The pupil is not the natural agent which the teacher uses; he is the consumer of that which the teacher produces, and, in practice, he, or others in his interest, pay the teacher for his product. The acquiring of instruction is the consumption of intellectual nourishment, as eating is of bodily nourishment; both are facilitated by the labor of attendants. There is a creation of minor form utilities in the carving of meat, the cutting of bread, etc., and of minor place utilities in the passing of plates and dishes. In the school-room there is a similar carving and cutting process in the assigning of lessons; the student takes his mental nutriment, like his physical, in portions adapted to his consuming capacity. As it would be absurd to say that the waiter and the cook find the product of their labor in a utility imparted to the body of the person who eats, so a similar absurdity exists in supposing that the teacher finds his product in a utility imparted to the mind of the one who learns. Both eating and learning are acts of consumption. They, in each case, result in a capacity to labor on the part of the consumer, but this personal endowment is not to be confused with the products which may, later, result from the exercise of it; working capacity is the natural result of assim-

ilating nutriment. The teacher is usually the waiter
at the intellectual table, while the cook is the author
of the text-books which he uses; it is, however, an aim
of higher education to unite these functions.

It is unnecessary to state that any natural agent not
originally wealth becomes wealth when it receives,
through the agency of labor or capital, either of the
four utilities above noticed. Air has place utility
when forced into a mine or a diving-bell. Water has
form utility in a fountain, place utility in a street
hydrant or watering cart, and time utility in the reservoir of a manufacturing village, where it is retained
for use during the dry season. If there are any products which, at first glance, appear as exceptions, they
are, on closer inspection, clearly seen to be illustrations of our definition of wealth. Some classes merit
more extended consideration than is here possible,
but it is believed that the above classification will be
found to cover the whole field of industrial labor.
Wherever human effort produces commodities, it will
be found to be conferring one of these four utilities on
a natural agent, or, in other words, to be subjecting
nature. This view is, singularly enough, presented
in a work that is old and familiar enough to have
well attracted the notice of those who have ransacked
the classics for fragmentary allusions to economic
science. In the picture of the origin of society found
in the book of Genesis, man is first represented in the

primitive paradisiacal state, conscious of no artificial
wants, and supplying his few natural wants from the
gratuitous productions of tropical nature. He eats of
the tree of knowledge, and, by this means, becomes
conscious of his simplest artificial want, and of the
necessity of supplying it by making nature serviceable. He passes to the state of actual development,
with the primitive paradise behind him and a restored
paradise, as the ever receding goal of his progress, in
the indefinite future before him, and it is here that
the injunction is laid upon him, or the law is written
within him, the fulfilment of which involves his whole
economic development, the command, namely, to " re-
plenish the earth and *subdue it.*"

CHAPTER III.

THE BASIS OF ECONOMIC LAW.

ECONOMIC laws depend on the voluntary action of men, and the science therefore professes, in effect, to teach how men will act under given circumstances. If prices rise, it is because some men choose to demand and others consent to give more money than formerly for the products of industry. To predict such a rise is to foretell the action of the human will. Assuming that the will is governed by desires, the metaphysical view most favorable to prediction, we still encounter the fact that the motives of human action are the ultimate determining forces, and that a misconception as to the nature of these motives is liable to vitiate any conclusion which may be attained. The value of the results of economic reasoning depends on the correctness of its assumptions with regard to the nature of man. If man is not the being he is assumed to be, there is no certainty that the conclusions will be even approximately correct.

It is more than can be here undertaken, to prove, by the analysis of leading works, that the motives attributed to men have been, in fact, erroneous.

That must be done by the reader for himself, by the study of those works. It is, however, believed and asserted that a candid reading of the literature of this subject will produce the conviction that writers have troubled themselves very little with anthropological investigation. Their attention has been employed, and well employed, elsewhere. They have assumed, as the basis of their science, a certain conception of man, and have employed their acuteness in determining what results will follow from the social labors of this assumed being. The premises have not been adequately verified; the system is, in so far, an ideal one, and it is, therefore, a matter of some chance whether its results are correct or not. Economic science has never been based on adequate anthropological study.

Inaccuracies in the science which result from inadequate conceptions of man are not to be rectified, as has been asserted, by a proper allowance for "disturbing forces." The actual course of a cannon-ball may be determined by a mathematical computation followed by the proper allowance for atmospheric resistance; but the social activities of men cannot be determined by assuming that man is a being of a certain kind, elaborating the conclusions with nicety, and then endeavoring to introduce the proper allowance for the fact that man is, after all, a being of quite a different kind. As Mr. Ruskin has well said, such disturbing influences are rather chemical than mechanical. "We made learned experiments upon pure nitrogen, and have convinced ourselves that it is a very manageable gas; but behold! the thing which we have practically to deal with is its chloride, and this, the moment we touch it on our established principles, sends us with our apparatus through the ceiling."

The only right course under such circumstances is to begin at the beginning and determine by investigation the nature of man, the subject under consideration; and this course should be adopted whether existing conclusions be true or false. The object is not so much to attain different results from those already reached, as to attain the same ones by a more legitimate method. The process which changes some false results will verify many true ones. The image which the scientist has constructed as the subject of his discussion may or may not resemble the man whom God has created; the latter only is the true subject of political economy. The science, which has rested on a temporary blocking of assumption, needs to be built on a permanent foundation of anthropological fact.

Having determined that the man of whom the economics of the past has treated is largely the creature of assumption, consideration will farther develop the fact that the assumed man does not, in fact, resemble the real one in several important respects, and that there is not only a possibility, but a moral certainty

that some erroneous conclusions have resulted from
this discrepancy. The assumed man is too mechanical and too selfish to correspond with the reality;
he is actuated altogether too little by higher psychological forces. What is true of a laboring machine
requiring only to be housed and clothed, and to be
fed, — that is, supplied with fuel as a motive power,
— will certainly not be altogether true of a laboring
man in modern society; and what is true of a being
whose affections, aspirations, and conscience are merged
in an abnormal love of acquisition will not be true
of those who accumulate and disburse fortunes in the
actual world.

The inadequate basis on which the traditional science rests is, in part, responsible for the growth of
the German Historical School, in which the laws of
wealth are sought by a study of recorded facts, rather
than by deduction from assumed premises. Yet he
must be ill informed who anticipates that, in the work
of this popular and growing school, deductive reasoning itself will fall into disuse. No one, perhaps, uses
such reasoning more acutely than Professor Karl Knies,
of Heidelberg, who deserves, as much as any one, the
credit of having given to the historical method a scientific standing. Logic must do its work, but its results must be verified. What is here claimed is that
its premises need first to be verified. The assumptions
of political economy need to be subjected to a com-

parison with facts. It is on its anthropological side that the traditional science is most defective, and it is by adequate studies in this direction that results may be attained which history will confirm. A broad field is thus opened for occupation. The first steps may be slow; it is easier to view a promised land from a mountain top than to capture it from the Canaanites. It is easy to take in at a glance the vast results that will follow from reconciling theory and practice in this department; but to trace the elusive laws of human nature, and to search through the maze of social facts without losing the grasp upon principles, will afford work enough for one generation.

What is here proposed is to point out this field, and then to cultivate it to a slight extent; it is to take from it, as it were, a first sod-crop, which will in nowise measure the ultimate fertility of the soil. It is proposed to consider certain facts relative to the nature of man, selecting those which require but little investigation, and which need only to be stated to be admitted, and, later, to apply these facts to some economic problems. If any light is thus thrown on questions now in doubt, if any new starting-point seems to be attained for future investigation, or if any modification results in economic principles as now understood, much greater and more valuable results may be expected from more extended inquiry. The simpler and more obvious the anthropological facts here

cited, and the more familiar the economic questions
to which they are applied, the stronger is the inference as to the ultimate value of completer anthropological studies. Such studies would give a new character
to political economy. They would verify its truths,
correct its errors, impart to it a kindly and sympathetic quality, and elevate it to a recognition of those
higher soul-forces which it has heretofore practically
ignored.

It is not merely man as an individual that needs to
be considered. A man is not independent. So close
is the relation between him and others of his race
that his conduct is dictated and his nature transformed
by it. Though a self-directing being of the highest
organization, he is made, by his relations to others, to
be an atomic portion of a higher organism, — society.

An organism is a living structure; and, though this
phrase suggests the need of formulating a definition
of that indefinable thing, life, it serves to distinguish
an organism from other structures. The parts of an
organism have been said to be so related that "each
is, at the same time, the means and the end of all the
others." The rootlet of a tree shares with the remote
leaf the nutriment which it absorbs from the earth,
and the leaf shares with the rootlet that which it
gathers from the sunlight and the air. This universal
interdependence of parts is a primary characteristic of
social organisms; each member exists and labors, not

for himself, but for the whole, and is dependent on the whole for remuneration. The individual man, like the rootlet, produces something, puts it into the circulating system of the organism, and gets from thence that which his being and growth require; he produces for the market, and buys from the market. Every producer is serving the world, and the world is serving every consumer.

The analogy between society and the human body was familiar to the ancients. It is a discovery of recent times that a society is not merely like an organism; it is one in literal fact. It is a late discovery that social organisms develop earliest in forms corresponding, not to man, but to the lower animals. The same characteristics which rank an animal as high or low in the scale of development give a similar rank to a society. Social organisms, like animal forms, are divided into four general classes, distinguished by precisely the same marks as those used in the biological classification. There are social vertebrates, articulates, mollusks, and radiates. The distinguishing marks are, first, differentiation, and, secondly, cephalization, or the subjection of the body to the control of the brain. The more unlike are the parts in form and function, and the more the structure is subjected to the directing influence of a thinking organ, the higher is the society in the scale of organic development.

Social differentiation is division of labor, a thing

which has but a rudimentary existence in the most
primitive tribes, which develops in the intermediate
types, and is carried to an indefinite extent in high civilization. In everything that can be termed a society
a traceable degree of interdependence exists among the
members; and, with advancing civilization, each member labors less and less for himself, and more and more
for the social whole. This is economic altruism, to the
future development of which no limits can be assigned.

The solidarity of society is a primary economic fact.
Political economy treats, not merely of the wealth of
individuals who sustain complicated relations with each
other, but of the wealth of society as an organic unit.
The production and the consumption of wealth by
society will be found to embrace its whole subject. The
world is before us with its resisting elements, the
"thorns and thistles" of Genesis; and we subdue it,
not by conquering each his little part, but by collectively subjugating all nature.

Society holds two distinct relations toward every
man; it is the object of his efforts; he is the object of
its efforts. He produces for the general market; it is
his study to ascertain a public want, and to create what
will supply it. He buys from the general market; he
informs himself concerning the goods of many producers, and buys wherever the things offered are
adapted in quality and price to his necessities. What
he consumes comes from every quarter of the earth.

Society is, thus, to be regarded as one party in every exchange that is made in the open market.

The social relation reacts on the nature of the individual. Man, the molecule of society, is transformed in his whole being by the unifying process of social development. The simple organism is made higher and better by becoming a part of the secondary organism. The changes which take place in different individuals vary according to the position which each assumes in the organic whole; the man who, in the development of society, becomes a molecule of the brain of the social organism undergoes widely different modifications in his own nature from those experienced by the man who becomes a molecule of the nutritive organ. The scientist differs in mental and physical development from the hand-worker. Apart from frivolous distinctions of caste, there exist classes founded on differences of social function, and accompanied by real differences in the individual.

Low organisms of every sort have few and simple wants. Primitive tribes, the mollusks and radiates of the social classification, have few wants in the aggregate, and their individual members have correspondingly few. Multiplicity of wants marks the grade of the society and of the individual. Simple food, little or no clothing, and the rudest of shelter suffice for the tropical savage; nomads require more varied appliances, and the civilized man demands an indefinite number and variety. Man, the consumer, acquires, through social development, an infinitude of conscious needs; and society, in its capacity of producer, diversifies its mechanism so as to supply them all. Society, as a consumer, develops an infinitude of wants; and man, as a producer, specializes his industrial action so as to assist in supplying one of them.

Closely connected with the growth of mere complication of social structure is the growth of specific vices and virtues. The isolated man had no neighbors to rob, and none to serve; his possibilities of evil and of good were limited. In the Mosaic picture the fruit, knowledge, the eating of which started Adam on a career of moral conflict, awakened in him the consciousness of his simplest artificial and distinctively social want, that, namely, of clothing, and introduced him to a life of labor. The growing complexity of the economic process has been accompanied by an increasing need of moral force, and by an increasing amount of it in actual operation. Social relations, wants and want satisfactions, sins and virtues multiply in corresponding degree. Together, therefore, with mere altruism, the economic principle by which man, in self-interest, is led to work for others, there grows, in controlling influence, the higher altruism of unselfishness. Society of the highest type is not merely differentiated and cephalized. There is, indeed, in high civilization, increasing division of labor,

and a progressive control of the social body by a thinking organ; but there exists, in as marked a degree,
a growing subordination of brain and members to the
dictates of moral law. This is the great and neglected
economic fact of modern times.

With the growth of ideal influences in society as a
whole, comes the chief transformation in individual
nature which is traceable to social influence. Men's
wants are not merely multiplied; they are spiritual-
ized.   Human desires extend themselves into scientific, æsthetic and ethical regions, and react directly
and powerfully on the production of wealth.   The
relative strength of the animal and the ideal wants in
different individuals is due, in part, to original endowment, and, in part, to acquirement; and this latter is
largely the result of social influences. He whose occupation it is to do much of the thinking of society
cultivates, perforce, his own intellectual nature; while
he who merely feeds or clothes it is under no such
elevating influence, and may suffer from a powerful
pressure in the direction of animal development. By
specializing the economic functions of men, society
specializes its influence on their nature.

Every man has his scale of wants, of varying intensity. The products of social industry appeal to him
with different degrees of power, from the food that
sustains his life, to the trifles that minister to his
caprices. Every man is subject to both the animal and

the spiritual desires. The most cultured is liable to hunger, and the rudest has some craving for knowledge and some appreciation of the beautiful. All have a sense of right. Where do the ideal wants fall in the scale of intensity? Does a man hunger for books somewhat as he hungers for bread, or does he place such objects among the luxuries or the superfluities? On the answer, in each man's case, depends the influence which he will exert on the economic action of society. The kinds of wealth produced and, as we shall see, the rates at which they are sold are largely determined by the acquired natures of men as consumers.

The lowest wants are susceptible of complete satisfaction; the higher are indefinitely expansive. Appetite ceases to act when sufficient nourishment has been taken, and the sense of cold, when the body has been sufficiently clothed. The pleasurable sense of taste is capable of less complete satisfaction; the savage eats long after hunger has ceased; and, even in civilized life, similar phenomena are observed. In like manner, the desire for personal adornment causes the wardrobe to be increased and varied long after the need of simple protection has been fully met.

Wants of this medium sort expand indefinitely, but decrease in intensity as the desired objects are supplied. Pleasures of this kind tend to cloy. The first gratification is an object of intenser desire than the second, and the second than the following. An indefinite number of such acquisitions would each afford some gratification, but in diminishing degree.

The highest wants are not only indefinitely expansive, but afford undiminished or increased gratification at each successive attainment of the objects of desire. The more a man knows, the more ardently he seeks knowledge and the things which secure knowledge. The more he enjoys of the beautiful, the more diligently he continues to seek it in art and nature. The better a man becomes, the more earnestly he strives after everything that tends to develop character. To the possible intensity of these supersensuous wants there is no assignable limit. A philosopher may forego the comforts of life for intellectual ends; and many men prefer a life of "plain living and high thinking" to the luxuries of philistinism. The love of right action, and the aspiration for worthy character may subordinate every lower impulse. But it is not merely in cases where the ideal motives overshadow all others that their presence is felt. They are a modifying influence in every man's conduct, and it is to their efficiency in society as a whole that all progress is due.

These ideal wants are all unselfish. The true and the beautiful are desired each for its own sake, and the desire for personal worthiness opposes self-interest as an equal antagonist. Under the influence of such motives, man can never be a being striving solely for personal advantage, and society can never be wholly

given over to an ignoble scramble for profit. These
motives, of course, find no place in a system of economies based on selfishness. At best they receive from
such a science a slighting recognition, as "disturbing
elements." Can such a system be maintained? Is
logic on its side, and is the opposition to it a matter
of sentiment? Do the hard facts of life sustain the
economic science which dehumanizes its subject? We
shall try to definitely answer these questions in later
chapters. The unselfish forces of society are doing
practical work. They create the altruism which gives
without return. It is not *do ut des*, but simply *do*,
where they are in control. They have filled the land
with schools, churches, art museums, hospitals and
numberless non-mercantile agencies for social improvement. They have diverted vast amounts of wealth
into ways of which no account can be taken in a system based on self-interest and limited to the field of
competition. They have, as we shall see, created a
practical department of non-competitive economies,
and are constantly enlarging its sphere by encroachments on the field where competition rules. If the
extreme and narrow view be taken that wealth in
process of disbursement is beyond the limits of economic study, this objection may be met upon its own
ground. It may be shown that the market itself is
permeated by moral influences, and that the competitive principle, instead of being supreme and resistless,

exists at best by sufferance, is subject to constantly narrowing restrictions, and is liable, in particular forms, to be totally suppressed by the action of that moral force which is, in reality, supreme.

A want that is universal and insatiable is the desire for personal esteem. It is a main spring of the energetic action on which the accumulation of wealth depends. It adjusts itself, in quality, to different natures, becoming low vanity or worthy ambition for public favor, according to the weakness or the strength of particular intellects. All men value their standing in the community, though they take different ways to secure it. It is this desire, in the main, that sets for each class a standard of living, and prompts them to effort to maintain it. It tends powerfully to elevate the condition of the poor, and is a main reliance of Malthusianism for the counteracting of that tendency to multiply in number which, if unchecked, would depress to the point of extreme hardship the condition of the laboring class. It is a chief incentive to the prodigal expenditures of the very wealthy; and at the same time, it impels to the accumulations which make large expenditures possible. It creates a limitless market for articles of decoration, and thus assists in giving a stable value to the precious metals, which are the basis of currency. Changes in the supply of whatever ministers to vanity are neutralized, in part, by the elasticity of the demand.

This desire is the basis of fashion, and, in this field of action, dominates the production of all form utilities into which an æsthetic element enters. Consumers and producers pay attention to its despotic dictates, since what is most saleable to-day may, by its influence, become a drug to-morrow.

That which most concerns us, in connection with this powerful economic force, is its action in supplementing the ideal motives of human nature. It counterfeits taste, intellect, and virtue where they have small existence. It causes low natures to resemble higher ones in their outward action, and elevates the general conduct of society toward the standard set by its best members. The newly made millionaire with no taste for art becomes a purchaser of paintings, meritorious or otherwise, according to his tact in utilizing the judgment of others in the selection. He fills his library with volumes ordered, possibly, according to shelf-room, by the linear foot independently of contents. In the acquisition of wealth the man whom virtue would not deter from fraud or robbery curbs his impulses from the love of commercial reputation. Mercantile honor has its roots in genuine morality; but its visible effects are multiplied by the love of personal esteem.

This desire not only counterfeits virtue in natures where it is lacking; it coöperates with it where it exists in full measure. The benevolence which founds colleges and hospitals is called out, in part, by their

monument-making character. There is much in the
name of a public institution. Yet the philanthropy
which disburses fortunes is not more assisted by this
worthy love of esteem than is the virtue which guards
men from contamination during the process of acquiring fortunes.

In the last analysis the sense of right in men is a
supreme motive, in the market as elsewhere. It is the
centripetal force in economic society. Its action is not
an occasional or "disturbing" influence; it is constant,
and increases with time and civilization. If classed as
a disturbing force, it promises eventually to overshadow
those classed as normal. There is, in fact, nothing
whatever of a disturbing nature about this motive; its
whole action tends to harmony. It is the one possible
means of realizing, in practice, those "economic harmo-
nies" which Messrs. Cary and Bastiat have thought
they perceived in the unrestrained action of selfish
motives. "Every man for himself" is the principle of
disorganization and chaos; "every man for mankind"
is the principle of organic unity. The more the action
of such motives increases, the more harmoniously and
rapidly will social development proceed, and the more
speedily will the highest activities of the individual man
be called forth. Such motives demand the first attention and the profoundest investigation. A truly scientific study of their action will afford the key to a
political economy that shall explain the facts of man's

present life, and give promise of a future that shall answer the cravings of his nature.

The wants of men are either latent or developed, according to their own intellectual condition, and according to the grade of culture of the society to which they belong. The ignorant man in a civilized state, and the primitive tribe as a whole, have, at best, but a latent desire for literature. Wants, when developed, admit of three distinct conditions, according to the possibility of gratifying them. The desire for what is decidedly beyond the possibility of attainment is not, in a healthy nature, either constant or active. The peasant passes the palace with indifference, and experiences, at most, a desultory and transient wish to be its occupant. Such a wish is a day-dream; it stimulates to no effort, and its non-fulfilment occasions little discontent. In passing a dwelling slightly better than his own the laborer may experience a desire of a different and more effective character. The desire for that which is attainable by effort is active, and stimulates to exertion in pursuit of the object. Failure in such a quest occasions lively disappointment. When the object has been attained, the want of it ceases, and the active desires extend themselves to remoter objects.

Wants admit of these three conditions; they are quiescent when the object of desire is unattainable, active when it is attainable, and in a different manner quiescent when it is attained. The first condition is

necessary to contentment, the second to ambition, and
the third to tranquil enjoyment. Contentment, ambition, and tranquil enjoyment are not inconsistent with
each other; but, on the contrary, the coëxistence of
these three mental states is the natural and healthy
condition of the mind. Despondency sometimes exists in fact, as other unhealthy conditions exist; but
it is not, in active life, the prevailing state. In a
community ordinarily prosperous men tend to contentment, hopefulness, and enjoyment, and the opposite conditions are the exceptions.

When combined with contentment, ambition furnishes the condition of healthy economic progress;
without it, it is an element of danger. A low grade
of contentment without ambition is the cause of the
security of caste-ruled despotisms. The safety of republics especially demands that, where this passion
exists, its development should be normal, that it should
strive after what is legitimately within reach and resign
what is beyond. It acts in this manner wherever
wealth is well distributed by a natural process, and
where the social system is not regarded as unsettled
and subject to change. Where wealth is ill distributed, and where the permanence of the social
system seems questionable, there are the conditions
of an abnormal ambition which is an element of
peril.

The mere possibility of revolution is a vitiating ele-

ment in the mental processes of men. It brings indefinite gains seemingly within the limits of attainment,
and undermines contentment. It renders those abnormal gains independent of labor, and palsies the
productive energies. It substitutes an eager and
hungry waiting for spoils for the healthy desire to
earn and to save wealth. It is the basis of deadly
enmity between social classes. The natural union of
contentment, hopefulness and tranquil enjoyment is
general only in those societies, the stability of which
is assured, and the industrial condition of which affords
to members of every class the opportunity for at least
a small amount of progress. The lazy and the improv-
ident may even then repine; but these are never a majority. For this reason a republic among whose people
communistic poison has begun its work should cling, as
a ship clings to its anchor, to whatever opens a door of
possible progress to the laboring class. It should give
more than a tolerant hearing to the theories of coöperation and profit-sharing, and should forgive many failures before rejecting them in practice. It should
treasure moral influences and everything that sup-
plements their action.

The leading English writers on political economy
have introduced a distinction between so-called "productive and unproductive consumption," the former
being the consumption of those things, the effect of
which is to enable a man to labor, and the latter, the

consumption of things which give simple gratification
without imparting laboring capacity. This distinction is of interest from the high authority on which
it rests, and from the important question which it is
sought to solve by its use. The economic effects of
luxury and of frugality are the real questions at issue
in the discussion of what is termed productive and
unproductive consumption. Mr. Mill conveys the impression of taking peculiar pleasure in this distinction,
and of conceiving that important light has been gained
by its use.

It is doubtless true that the employment of this
distinction for the purpose indicated is unnecessary,
and that it involves some confusion of thought. Pro-
fuse expenditure differs from frugal living, not in
producing less wealth, but in destroying more. In
itself consumption is never productive, but is usually
more or less destructive. A certain kind of consumption is supposed, by its reaction upon the energies of
man, to result in a subsequent creation of wealth.

It would doubtless be conceded by those who use
this distinction that it is impossible to rigidly apply
it in actual life. To draw a line between that which,
when consumed, gives capacity for labor, and that
which does not, is impracticable. Comforts, as well
as necessities, may increase the ability to work, and
necessities, as well as comforts, may give gratification.
The food of nearly every man satisfies wants higher

in the scale than that of simple nourishment; it gives a sensuous gratification distinct from its nutritive action. The clothing of every one above destitution satisfies higher wants than those of warmth and protection, those, namely, of personal adornment and of social consideration. So with the dwelling, and the entire surroundings. It is impossible to say that food, clothing, and shelter are productively consumed, or even that distinguishable portions of them are so.

To consume only productively one must eat the cheapest food that will adequately nourish, wear the simplest clothing that will completely protect, and live in the rudest dwelling that will fully shelter. All higher wants must remain unsatisfied, and the man must become a machine, content with the fuel that keeps him in motion. Here is the chief weakness of the classification, and the reason for mentioning it in this connection; — to make a man a machine is to make him anything but productive.

That such a result can never be realized in fact is self-evident; that it should ever be conceived of in thought is an evidence of how little trouble even the greatest writers on political economy have given themselves concerning the real nature of the being with whose actions they deal. If the laborer is an engine, his motive power is fuel; if he is a man, his motive power is hope. It is psychological rather than physiological forces which keep him in motion. His will, and not merely his muscle, is an economic agent, and he is to be lured, not pushed, in the way of productive effort. Ambition may have feeble sway in individual cases, but, this side of the gate of Dante's Inferno, it is never entirely extinct.

We have seen that wants on the margin of actual possession are the active incentives to effort. Civilized man struggles no longer for existence, but for progressive comfort and enjoyment. It is the hope of small and legitimate gains which makes general contentment possible; the absence of it breeds a sullen submission to hardship, tempered, in many cases, by dreams of communistic plunder.

Progress has limits, and many wants must remain forever unsatisfied. By a kindly provision of human nature, such wants are generally quiescent. Other wants near to the border line of actual possession must be active, with a prospect of satisfaction by effort, if happiness is to be attained. It is the want of things which lie far above the line of necessities, and the consumption of which would be classed as unproductive, which is the constant motive power in industrial progress. The comforts to be enjoyed to-morrow set in action the muscular energy gained by the food consumed to-day. It is the so-called "unproductive consumption" which, if soul forces be recognized, is productive of wealth.

The ultimate foundations of political economy lie deeper than the strata on which existing systems have been reared. The point of divergence between the present science and the true science lies farther back than ordinary inquiries extend. The economist of the future must begin at the beginning of all knowledge, and, with Socrates, pass through the portal from which diverge the various walks of scientific inquiry, and over which the master has written "γνῶθι σεαυτόν." Self-knowledge is the beginning of every science; but it is a peculiarly comprehensive self-knowledge that is the basis of the coming economic system. Knowledge of men is the beginning of this science; knowledge of the social organism of which men are members is the middle and the end of it. Individual desires are molecular forces in the general life of society, and to them all phenomena of wealth must be ultimately traced. It is by a deeper analysis than has been dreamed of in our philosophy that we may hope to attain that higher insight, that knowledge first of man, and then of humanity, which is the basis of true economics.

CHAPTER IV.

THE ELEMENTS OF SOCIAL SERVICE.

MEN are altruistic in their economic action; society is egoistic. Men work for each other; society works for itself. For many purposes the most available conception of the entire economic process is that of the social organism as a producer, laboring to serve each individual member as a consumer.

Wealth is the means by which society serves its members. Resolving social service into effort and gratification, we find, as in our former analysis, an outward and material connecting link between them. One man's effort gratifies another man through the medium of some specific product; the effort of society gratifies all its members through the medium of all products. Serving is creating social wealth, and being served consists in consuming it.

Production and consumption, the primary elements of social service, are the reverse of each other in every particular. Man acts on nature in the one process; nature on man in the other. Utilities come into existence through the sacrifices of men, and, as a rule, pass out of existence in the process of promoting their welfare.

Consumption is utilization, and the destruction of the object consumed is, in most cases, an unhappy attendant circumstance of the process. It is not its essential element; most utilities are of such a nature that they exhaust themselves, slowly or rapidly, as the case may be, in producing their effect on men. Yet one form of wealth, land, which is not created by labor, is not destroyed in utilization. It may be improved or injured to an indefinite extent; utilities may be added to it or taken from it; but to create or to destroy space on the surface of the earth is beyond human power. The primary service rendered by land is that of affording standing ground and travelling room; although in nearly every locality short of the poles or the deep sea, it has an ultimate capacity to become a food producer. A man utilizes or consumes land when he stands on it or drives across it. He consumes a mountain when he causes it to lift him a thousand feet into the air, and to afford a view of the river valley. In another way he consumes the valley itself by looking upon it and enjoying its beauty. The attractions of a landscape are utilities, and to enable them to produce their effect on the human sensibility is one mode of consumption.

Wealth is commonly and accurately termed "means"; utilization is the end to which it corresponds. Maximum utilization is the goal of the economic process, the *summum bonum* of social economy. The mere quantitative increase of wealth is, indeed, a factor in that result; but it is one factor only. The greatest social wealth does not necessarily create the greatest social weal; that result depends, in a great degree, on the quality and the distribution of the weal-constituting element. The securing of the greatest quantity, the highest quality, and the most equitable distribution of wealth is the rational goal of economic society. How much this involves we shall later see.

In a loose sense production and consumption overlap each other in time; in a more accurate sense they are completely distinct, and the terminal point of the one process marks the initial point of the other. The difference lies in the two uses of the word consumption.

The desire for a useful object induces a secondary desire for whatever may become a means of securing it. The need of a dwelling for shelter induces a secondary desire for the stone, brick, and lumber that will compose it, and, again, for the trees that will furnish the lumber, the quarries that will furnish the stone, etc. If the gratification of these mediate wants be regarded as a subordinate variety of utilization, then production and consumption are jointly in progress in most industrial operations. The utilizing of trees is the production of lumber, and that of lumber is the production of houses. The ultimate end is the direct gratification of a want of man's nature. Production continues till that goal is reached; final utilization, or true consumption begins at that point; but secondary consumption may be traced backward through all the steps by which the goal is approached. Every step that brings us nearer to the end satisfies a mediate desire. It may not be illogical to apply the term consumption, as is commonly done, to this secondary utilization; but it is illogical to fail to distinguish its peculiar quality, and to neglect to use a qualifying adjective to mark the distinction. Consumption in the full sense is that final utilization which is distinct from production in time, and the opposite of it in quality.

In this use of terms the production carried on by society as an organic whole includes the process of exchange, and involves that of distribution. The four traditional divisions of economic science are not distinct and coördinate. In the very act of completing a product society passes it many times from hand to hand. One producer, or group of producers digs ore, another smelts it, another rolls the metal, another cuts it, with the result that society has produced, perhaps, a keg of nails. Each step in the process has involved a transfer of products, and the end is marked by an exchange of a different kind. In this last exchange the act by which society disposes of a product completed and ready for final utilization may be regarded as the terminal act of social production. The acquiring of that product by the user may, in like manner, be classed as the initial act of consumption.

Division of labor specializes man's productive action in two ways. There is, first, a broadly qualitative division of labor, which assigns to an extensive group of producers the creation of a single complete product, like the keg of nails above referred to. A subdivision assigns each of the general steps in the process to a subordinate group. Mining, smelting, rolling, and cutting are performed by specialists, who, in each case, give to the material the particular transformation which they have learned to impart, and pass it to the next workers in the series. "Touch and pass on" is the social order; and each transformation adds to the material a particular increment of utility, a sub-product, as we shall later have occasion to term it. The creation by society of any complete product involves a series of exchanges between the producers of the sub-products; and these transfers are integral parts of the general productive operation.

Where several distinct operations are performed in a single manufacturing establishment, there are, of course, no exchanges between the groups of workmen who perform them. Spinning, weaving, and dyeing are mechanically distinct processes; but spinners in a mill do not sell their product to the weavers, and these, again, to the dyers. Yet sales do, in effect, take place here. These sales are unique in quality, and stand in a direct

relation to distribution. The sellers are all the workmen; the only buyers are the employers, and the result
of the sale is a division between these parties of the
value which the mill creates. The full discussion of
this transaction is reserved for the chapter on wages.

Logically exchange and distribution are distinct from
each other; practically they are merged. The same
series of acts performs both functions. Exchanges are
specific transactions between individuals; distribution
is a general process performed by society as a whole.
It is a division of the income of society among its members, and is effected by means of all the interchanges of
products which take place between individuals.

As ordinarily defined, exchange and distribution are
not even logically distinct. Scientific treatment demands that the logical separation, at least, shall be
maintained; and it may be so by rational definitions.
Exchange is a qualitative diffusion of wealth; distribution is a quantitative diffusion. Exchanges determine
in what concrete things a man's wealth shall embody
itself; distribution determines how much of that wealth,
in abstract quantity, there shall be. If a farmer, having
surplus wheat, sells it for an equivalent in clothing and
implements, his wealth changes its form of embodiment,
but not its amount. His assets acquire a new character
by his visit to the market, but the inventory shows the
same sum total as before.

Yet there is something in the sales constantly going

on in society which has the effect of determining what
commodities are to be regarded as, in abstract value, the
equivalents of each other. This influence has assigned
to the farmer's wheat a certain purchasing power, fixed
the quantity of clothing and implements which he can
get for it, and, by this means, determined his share in
the general wealth of society. This determining influence is the adjustment of ratios of exchange in the
general market.

An exchange involves, first, a bargain, and secondly,
a double transfer of commodities. The bargain involved in the transfer is not a part of it. The fixing
of the rate at which two commodities shall be exchanged is antecedent to the act which changes the
ownership of the articles. The fixing of a rate of
exchange is an act in social distribution, while the
double transfer of the commodities themselves is all
that, in the last analysis, there is in the process of
exchange. The establishment of market prices for
everything determines every producer's share in the
varied results of social industry, and, as already
stated, is identical with the process of social distribution. If the fixing of rates be not, in the discussion, kept sharply distinct from the mere change
of ownership of the commodities themselves, then the
term exchange can have no definiteness of meaning.
If the distinction be made, and if the term be applied
to the rate-adjusting operation, it becomes the name

of the transaction by means of which society as a
whole divides its income. Exchange in general means,
thus, distribution analyzed into its ultimate acts, and
regarded from an individualistic point of view.

In the strict use of terms an exchange reduces
itself to a double alienation and a double acquisition of concrete commodities. "I give," "I take,"—
acts of will made known in the briefest speech, are
the essence of the double transfer. These acts require but an instant of time, and no effort but that
of communicating the result. Time may have been
consumed in reaching a decision, and effort in adjusting terms. That part of the conversation between
a buyer and a seller which consists in discussing the
quality of goods has in view an adaptation of products to the needs and tastes of a consumer. It
resolves potential utilities into actual ones. It causes
an article which is capable of rendering a service to
actually render it to the user, and is a part of the
general process of mercantile production.

We shall consider later the fact that actual exchanges
are not always for equivalents, and shall endeavor to
place in its proper category that margin of illegiti-
mate profit which a shrewd trader may make both in
buying and in selling. He who parts with ten units
of value and receives twenty accomplishes, in fact, an
exchange, and a fraud or a robbery besides.

The bargaining processes which determine the selling

price of finished products in the market stand in a less
direct relation to distribution than do those which
adjust wages; the latter divide a value between employers and employed. Wages are, as we shall demon-
strate, payments for a certain kind of product; the
agreement to work for an employer is a contract on the
laborer's part to sell his future interest in the product
which his labor will assist in creating. The man who
agrees to run a sewing-machine in a shoe manufactory
contracts, in effect, to acquire and to sell an undivided
share in the shoes. This bargain determines the return
of his labor more directly, though not more really, than
the later transactions which determine the value of the
shoes as completed and offered in the market.

The primary elements of social service are, then, the
production and the consumption of wealth by the social
organism as a whole. Exchanges, or double transfers of
commodities, are integral parts of social production.
The adjustment of rates of exchange constitutes, in the
aggregate, the process of distribution. This is a dividing of wealth, in abstract quantity, among individuals,
and is incidental to production and consumption by
society.

Competition is a term commonly made to include the
entire process of adjusting rates of exchange, and thus
of determining distribution. It is described as a war-
fare, and when looked at in its entirety, presents, in
fact, the semblance of an indiscriminate *melée*, in which

the element of strife predominates. It is not, however, a blind contest; there is a method in it, the analysis of which is as important as any study in practical economics. Strife is increasing in our times because true competition is diminishing. That which was the basis of Ricardian economics is slowly passing out of existence at points where its presence is most needed, leaving society in a condition anomalous, full of peril, and demanding a prompt recourse to a new principle of adjustment in the distributing of the rewards of industry.

What is loosely termed competition consists, first, of a rivalry for public favor, resembling, not a battle, but a race; and, secondly, of a bargaining process having the capacity to become a quasi-combat. The former element only is true competition, and, where it is present, it affects the contest which follows, and takes the greater part of the belligerency out of it.

Ten men offer similar articles in the market, and we buy from one of them: but we have no words with him. If he demands too much, we shall buy from another; he knows this, and the knowledge forestalls the excessive demand. The tacit recognition of the presence of several buyers, on the one hand, and of several sellers, on the other, is a substitute for much argument. In retail traffic bargains are made with a minimum of "higgling"; the competition preceding actual purchases takes away the root of strife.

It is where the efforts of rivals to outdo each other
in serving the public are wanting that strife ensues.
Without the steadying effect of true competition a
bargain becomes a contest of strength in which one
man's gain is another man's loss, a transaction which
is liable to strain the personal relations of the participants, and even to render them surly or desperate, in
cases where vital interests are involved. The determining influences in such crude adjustments of value
are shrewdness and ultimate endurance ; and a man
does not take a defeat by either method with equa-
nimity. Still less do classes of men do so when the
issue determines their means of livelihood and comfort.

Such is coming to be the situation in the relations
of capital and labor. A contest is here in process on
a scale of magnitude impossible in earlier times, a
battle in which organized classes act as units on the
respective sides. The solidarity of labor on the one
hand, and of capital on the other, is the great economic
fact of the present day; and this growing solidarity is
carrying us rapidly towards a condition in which all
the laborers in a particular trade and all the capitalists
in that trade, acting, in each case, as one man, will
engage in a blind struggle which, without arbitration,
can only be decided by the crudest force and endurance. The strained relations of the parties in the
contest, the surliness and desperation, the threatenings
of literal war, are already the phenomena of it. The

essential peril to society lies in no superficial features, such as rifle-clubs and dynamite laboratories, but in the fundamental change that has taken place in the economic relations of the parties. The competitive principle has been vitiated. The strife-allaying element, the healthy rivalry on either side, has yielded to solidarity, which is rapidly growing. Already the hope is openly expressed of such a union of all labor that a universal strike may become possible if not actual.

To what, then, is a system once supposed to be nothing if not competitive actually tending? To the annihilation of competition at the point where its strife-allaying action is most needed. The rivalry between large producers and small ones has centralized capital, and substituted production by a few great firms and corporations for that which was formerly carried on in numberless little shops. The reduction of the number of establishments has made producers' unions possible, effecting monopolies in many directions, and thus partially destroying that variety of competition which formerly fixed the prices of completed products in the market. The aggregations of capital have given a one-sided character to transactions between employers and employed. A corporation owning a village, and with no present competitor, must hold at great disadvantage a thousand laborers who, in dull times, underbid each other for employment. Under such circumstances

Cobden's formula for a rise of wages, "two bosses after one man," could scarcely be realized; but his formula for a fall of wages, "two men after one boss," would describe a somewhat constant condition. Indeed, could the supposed case become actual, could the competition of capitalists in other villages be completely excluded, and could all unions of laborers be prevented, then wages might perhaps be adjusted according to a formula which barons under the feudal system employed in dealing with their subjects; they might be gauged "*ad misericordiam*," according to the dictates of a compassion which, in a corporation, might or might not exist.

The supposed case is a highly ideal one. Competition on the employers' part has never been excluded; and on the other hand labor unions have long been actively at work. With the tendency to consolidation on the side of capital, such unions become inevitable and right. Yet they oppose to the solidarity of capital a solidarity of labor, make wage adjustments to be bargains between two parties without rivalry on either side, and threaten to introduce into the industrial system an element of strife for which there is no analogy in anything which appears in a system truly competitive, and which, for possible brutality, may perhaps be accurately likened to a club contest of two cave-dwelling men. It is Ricardianism, the competitive system duly "let alone," the natural action of self-interest in men, that has brought us face to face with this condition.

Can an organic unity grow out of a principle of strife? The answer is obvious; and the inference is that competition, as it has existed, is not a principle of strife. Distribution by a bargaining process without true competition is something by which no society could have developed. The general adoption of this method no society can survive. The strife already created by it is rending the social organism, and would ultimately destroy it but for one redeeming fact, — the certain advent of a new principle of distribution. This social force is new only in its mode of operation ; fundamentally it is the same moral force that, when the competitive system was at its best, was, in reality, supreme in the economic life of men. We shall examine its working in the following chapters, a study which must begin with an analysis of the nature of Value, and of the laws that govern ratios of exchange in the general market.

CHAPTER V.

THE THEORY OF VALUE.

THE charm of novelty, at least, should attach to a philosophy of value, provided only that it prove to be the true one; for it is certain that in all that has been written on this much elucidated theme, a statement of the real nature of the thing discussed is not to be found. One cause of this marked deficiency is to be sought in the incomprehensive view which writers have taken. The great fact that society is an organic unit has been, for the time, forgotten, and the attention has been fixed on individuals and their separate and intricate actions in valuing and exchanging commodities. It is as though the physiologist, instead of studying the human body as a whole, were to confine his attention to the microscopic activities of the separate molecules that compose it. Intricate and nearly profitless would be such a study, and far too intricate and profitless has been the study of the department of social physiology comprehended under the theory of value. This subject can never be grasped and understood until the organic whole is made the primary object of attention. The value theory must receive the benefit of late studies in social science. The conception of society as an organism must be applied to this question, which, of all questions of political economy, is most dependent on the comprehensive view thus gained. Then only will our theories cease to lose themselves in the intricate tracing of individual activities, which is only social microscopy.

Who has not learned to his sorrow, how unsatisfying, in fact, are such discussions of value as claim to be particularly scientific, and how large a mass of literature he may patiently read through without satisfying himself exactly what value is? Aside even from its want of comprehensiveness, the reader will find the prevailing mode of discussion leading to specific difficulties and contradictions, from which he would give much to be delivered. He will learn that utility has something to do with value, that it is, indeed, included in the popular meaning of the word; but he will be enjoined to break with this popular notion, and, in science, to limit the meaning of the general term to something formerly called value in exchange. Yet, while encouraged to interpose as wide a gulf as is possible between value proper and utility, the reader will, on the other hand, find that he is allowed to confound utility with something once termed value in use. He will find that definitions are attempted of the two varieties of value, separately considered; but he may search economic literature in vain for a satisfactory formula for value in the generic. What value is, whether in use or exchange, few have attempted to tell us at all, and none have told us in a manner that is clear and satisfying.

Yet who supposes that a universal popular idea is baseless? Who would claim that the subtle intuitions that determine the ordinary use of terms are not a guide to scientific truth? If men continue, in spite of instructions, to use one term where the economist uses two, it is evidence that, in some way, the thing signified must be generically one; that there is, in the seemingly dual idea, a unity which the scientist has not as yet grasped. If the notion of utility, of usefulness, persists in attaching itself to the word value, whenever used in common speech, it is certain that there is a closer connection between them than has yet been detected. Latin *valeo*, French *valeur*, English *value*, as well as other foreign synonymes, all include the idea of usefulness, whatever else they may signify; and a formula that will harmonize with this permanent usage, and express the meaning of the term in any connection, is what the mind instinctively craves.

With due apology for the audacity of the attempt, and a consciousness of its difficulty, I am about to hazard the effort to obtain a comprehensive view of value, and to formulate a definition that shall express the fundamental thought which is present whenever the term is used. Instead of finding that utility is something necessary, indeed, to the existence of value, but not included in its proper meaning, something which we must drop out of mind as we become very scientific, we shall find that utility and value are inseparably bound in thought, and that the attempt to dissociate them betrays a failure on the part of the scientist to follow, with his analysis, the subtle mental processes that have determined the popular mode of expression, and given the public a truer notion of value than science has yet attained.

Value is an abstract term, and analysis will show that the abstraction is not a primary one. The notion is not formed by fixing the thought exclusively on one of the qualities that make up our conception of some concrete thing. Such a process may be termed a primary abstraction. The resulting notion, the quality itself, may become the basis of a secondary or higher abstraction. The quality may have attributes, and one of these may be made the object of thought. As the primary process gave us an attribute of a concrete thing, the secondary process gives us an attribute of an attribute. Certain things are useful, and a primary act of abstraction presents to the mind the quality, utility. This quality may exist in different degrees; some things are more useful than others. To determine how useful a thing is, is to measure its

utility. Quantitative measure, then, is an attribute
of the quality, utility. The fixing of the thought
exclusively on this attribute is the secondary process
of abstraction; it gives us the notion, *measure of
utility*, and it is this that I propose maintaining as
the true formula for value in the generic. Value is
quantitative measure of utility. Always and everywhere there is present to the mind that makes a valuation, whether for use or exchange, the conception
of a concrete thing, of a quality of that thing, and of
the quantitative measure of that quality.

Value and utility are, therefore, as inseparable as a
measure and that which is measured. The conception of linear extension could be as logically separated
from the conception of a geographical mile, as the idea
of utility from that of value.

On the other hand, value and utility are no more to
be confounded with one another than separated; two
inseparable things are not one thing. A measure and
that which is measured are not identical. The metal
lying on the scales possesses the quality, weight; that
general quality is not identical with the fact that the
weight amounts to just a hundred pounds. The
quality is not to be confounded with the quantity of
the quality. Utility is never identical with value,
either in use or exchange.

Still less is value to be confounded with the expression for it; that would be confusing the result of a

measurement with the object used by the measurer to convey that result to another mind. A unit of linear extension is not identical with a foot-rule, nor a unit of weight, with a metal disc that weighs a pound. Place a quantity of nails on one arm of the scales, and a metal disc on the other. The scales swing freely; the nails are weighed. Are we in danger of saying that the metal disc *is* the weight of the nails? We say that two weights are equal. There is a common quality in two objects, and the measure of that quality is the same in both. Unless very undiscriminating, we shall not say that a metal disc of smaller and finer sort, a dime, for instance, *is* the value of the nails. There is a quality common to nails and disc, and the measure of that quality is the same in both.

We need to pause but a moment to distinguish value from price; the latter is a mode of expressing value. All measurements are expressed by comparisons. In the rude beginnings of mensuration there is no unit of linear extension, and the length of an object is vaguely expressed in terms of anything that chances to be near it. When a common unit is adopted, say the length of a human foot of rather prehistoric proportions, measurements are expressed in terms of that common standard. Extension is the same, whether expressed in vague general comparisons, or in feet and inches. Values are expressed in vague general comparisons until the adoption of a unit for measuring utility; utility is the same whether expressed in the ruder or the more accurate way. Measure of utility expressed in terms of a conventional unit is price.

If the essential distinctions have now been clearly made; if concrete things, a quality of those things, the measure of that quality and the conventional expression for that measure are each so distinct from all the others that there is no danger of confusing them, we are prepared to advance to the essential argument, and prove, if possible, that value is, in fact, always a measure of utility. For it occurs to us at the outset — and, if it did not, any text-book of political economy would remind us — that things having widely different degrees of apparent utility have the same value in the market. We remember the diamond and the water of Adam Smith's illustration, and his assertion, true in spite of criticism, that the gem, the costliest of articles, satisfies a want much less intense than that satisfied by the water, which costs little or nothing. Is our theory stranded at the outset?

We must now make a distinction which, so far as I am aware, has never before been applied in political economy,* but one which, as I hope to show, is absolutely essential to clear reasoning in this department of the science. The conception of utility itself, unanalyzed, is misleading. Simple as the term apparently is,

* This chapter was published as a review article, in July, 1881.

there are two widely different meanings in it, and a value theory leads to directly opposite results, according as, in the use of terms, the one or the other is adopted. What is utility? Evidently a capacity to serve, a power to satisfy wants. To satisfy wants is to change the condition of the person served, to bring him from a lower degree of happiness to a higher. Without the useful object the man, for the time being, is in one condition; with it he is in another. The power thus to modify subjective conditions is utility; the difference between the two conditions affords the measure of that utility, that which we have termed value. In the measuring process, or mental valuation, the man reasons: "Without this article my condition, for a time, would be thus; with it, it is thus; the difference measures the utility of the object."

The cubic mile of air about your dwelling sustains your life; of course it has infinite utility. But has it? Annihilate it and see. Other air at once takes its place, and your condition remains unaltered. Under actual circumstances that particular volume of the life-sustaining gases appears not to have the power to modify your condition. Contrast your present state with your state if there were no air, and you find an indefinitely wide difference; contrast your present state with that in which the annihilation of that particular volume, and of no other, would have left you, and you find no difference at all.

The one mode of estimating gives a measure of what may be termed absolute utility; and, in the case of air, this is indefinitely great. The other estimate measures what may be termed effective utility; and, in the case of air, this is nothing. Effective utility is, then, power to modify our subjective condition, under actual circumstances, and is mentally measured by supposing something which we possess to be annihilated, or something which we lack to be attained.

Now, is not this the utility with which political economy has to deal; and is not the former, or absolute utility, that with which actual treatises have dealt? Moreover, is not the difference radical, and the failure to distinguish it ruinous to any philosophy? Air is not wealth, we have been taught, solely because no one can own it. True, of the atmosphere as a whole; but cannot a man own some of it? Let him but close doors and windows, and he will have it. There it is, in sufficiently complete possession, and undoubtedly useful, in the prevalent sense of the term. In consistency we should term it wealth. It is not so; and we know it; and our analysis reveals what is lacking, — effective utility. The presence or absence of the particular volume appropriated is indifferent to us, under actual circumstances; the presence of an indefinite supply, ready to replace it, destroys its importance. It is always in view of actual circumstances that we make our economic estimate; and it is effective, and not absolute utility that is the basis of wealth and value. Absolute utility may, for present purposes, be forgotten.

The measurement of effective utility in our illustration was simple; but it is not in common practice, a comparison of two simple conditions that is presented to the mind when mental valuations are made. The problem is more complicated, though not so complex as to be difficult of analysis. A few typical cases will sufficiently illustrate the principles involved. Air in a closed dwelling was effectively valueless, because its withdrawal caused no inconvenience; the owner's condition was the same before and after the withdrawal. Remove the drinking water from the table before him, and you modify his status; it becomes needful that he refill the glasses, and the sacrifice necessary to ensure the refilling, in whatever form that sacrifice may be made, is to be regarded as a subtraction from the sum total of his gratifications. If we could attain a unit for the measuring of happiness, it would be a compound standard like the foot-pound of mechanics, units of intensity multiplied by units of time. Applying such a standard, too ethereal, indeed, for practical use, to the condition of the man in our illustration, we should find that his day's enjoyment had been lessened by the withdrawal of the water. It did not remain wanting, but was immediately restored; yet the restoring process itself caused a lessening of the sum of our supposed subject's gratifications. The difference between the

present sum of his enjoyments, and the sum of enjoyments, had the removal not taken place, measures the
effective utility of the water. Let us examine a third
and last typical case, and suppose that the water
removed was replaced by that which was less refresh-
ing and serviceable. There are now two modifications
of the owner's subjective status, one caused by the sacrifice of replacing the water, and another by the inferi-
ority of that which was brought in its stead. His sum
of gratifications is twice lessened ; the measure of the
effective utility of the water is determined, exactly as
before, by comparing his present sum of gratifications
with that which he would have attained had the removal and replacement not taken place.

Now it is estimates like these that are actually made,
in measuring the utility of commodities. There is at
hand a well from which to draw,— a general market ;
and the removal of any article modifies a man's condition as the removal of the water, in our illustration
— he must replace the article by a sacrifice, and he
may or may not replace it completely. If he replaces
it completely, there is but one subtraction from the
sum of his enjoyments ; if he replaces it but partially,
there are two. In any case the resultant modification of his subjective status entailed by the removal
of the article measures its effective utility. The removal of a coat lessens the owner's enjoyment, not
by the difference between his condition with such a

garment and his condition with none, but by the difference between the sum of his enjoyments, had the coat not been taken, and the sum after the necessary sacrifice shall have been made to replace it, and the substitute, perfect or imperfect, shall have been brought into use.

An individual man may make all these measurements; value is possible, indeed inevitable, in a condition of isolation. Crusoe compared utilities with one another, though, having no bargains to make, he was under the less necessity of forming accurate estimates; and men, in society, make such estimates independently. A measurement of utility made by an individual gives value in use, not at all identical with what passes under that name in current discussion, which is utility itself, but the quantitative measure of that utility to an individual user. We have now to see that, in a sense, measurements of utility are never made by any other than a single independent being. Society, as an organic whole, is to be regarded as one great isolated being; and this being may and does measure utilities like a solitary tenant of an island. This great personage is complex; it has collections of men as its members, and single men as its molecules; and in studying the internal activities that take place when the valuations are in process, we shall be led into a sort of higher or social physiology, which will develop farther than has yet been done the parallelism existing between the individual and the social organism. It is from this source that, as was stated above, we are to derive our chief light on the philosophy of value. After the comprehensive view has been attained and the general movements of the social body traced, we may adopt, with advantage, the analytical method, fixing the attention on individuals, and finding how they deal with their neighbors. This is social microscopy.

Market value is a measure of utility made by society considered as one great isolated being; market price is, of course, that measure expressed in terms of a common standard. If the market value of a ton of coal and that of a barrel of flour are equal, it signifies that society, as an organic whole, estimates their respective utilities alike; if the prices of the coal and the flour are the same, it signifies that society has measured their utilities by a common standard, and expressed the measurements alike, in terms of that standard.

We need to be detained but a moment by the difficulty that, if a loaf of bread is worth, in the market, only a small fraction of a gem, all the loaves in the world would be worth but a few gems; while they possess indefinitely greater effective utility. It is essential to their present market value that they be offered and estimated separately. Were they owned and offered as a whole, their value would be indefinitely greater. Let some bold and successful monopolist effect what he would term a "corner" in bread, and its value would indefinitely exceed that of all the gems in existence.

More serious, in appearance only, is the fact of the vast service, under actual circumstances, which many low-priced articles render. How measureless is the utility, effective as well as absolute, of the poor man's loaf! Its removal might starve him, though another were to be had for a dime.

It is society, not the individual, that makes the estimate of utility which constitutes a social or market valuation. That is a part of our definition, — measure of service rendered to society as an organic whole. Though the thing were priceless to its owner, it might be cheap to society.

But the owner is a part of the social body, and is the organic whole indifferent to his suffering? If so, society is an imperfect and nerveless organism. It ought to feel, as a whole, the sufferings of every member, and what makes or mars the happiness of every slightest molecule, should make or mar the happiness of all.

A sympathetic connection between members of society exists, and prompts to the relief of suffering; a sense of right also exists, and moves the social organism more powerfully in the same direction. It results from these influences that poor-laws are enacted and alms-houses established, and that the man whose

last obtainable loaf has been destroyed may call upon
a social agency to replace it. The loss entails upon
the social body a minute expenditure of labor, a slight
sacrifice in the replacement, and this, by the terms
of our definition, gauges the importance of the loaf to
society. The question upon what members of the
social body the loss of wealth shall fall, is distinct
from the question how great is that loss itself; the
latter question determines the social estimate of
effective utility, which fixes market value; the former
question is one of equity in the internal arrangement
of society. Within its own membership the social organism adjusts losses on equitable principles, throwing
them, in the case of a pauper, first on a local community, and then on its individual members in proportion to their taxes. In any case the loss of a necessary article entails upon the social whole the necessity of diverting a quantity of labor from other productive directions, and this sacrifice gauges the market
value of the article.

The social organism is never nerveless; independently of sympathy between man and man, there is
a beautiful law of society as a whole, which makes
the wants of every member a matter of decisive interest to all. It is society as a whole that originally
bought the loaf from its producer; in a sense, it
bought it for the poor man, and for him only, and
would never think of taking it from him. Parents

would not take away a child's toy, not merely because
of affection, but because of the adaptation of the toy
to the child's use. Acting for the family as a whole,
they bought the plaything for the child, and to transfer it to themselves would lessen its service to the
family. Independently of personal sympathies, society
assumes a paternal relation toward particular members, buys articles for their use, consigns the articles
to them, and has no desire to take them again.

Exchanges are always made between an individual
and society as a whole. In every legitimate bargain
the social organism is a party. Under a regime of
free competition, whoever sells the thing he has produced, sells it to society. His sign advertises the
world to come and buy, and it is the world, not the
chance customer, that is the real purchaser. Yet it
is equally true that whoever buys the thing he
needs, buys it of society. Under free competition
the world is seeking to serve us, and we buy what the
world, not a chance producer, offers.

When market valuations are made, society is primarily the buyer. Goods in individual hands are offered
to the social whole, and the estimate of utility made
by that purchaser fixes their market value. In the
process the social organism is true to its nature as a
single being, great and complex, indeed, but united
and intelligent. It looks at an article as a man would
do, and mentally measures the modification in its own

condition which the acquisition of it would occasion, or which the loss of it would occasion, if once possessed. "With the article my condition is thus; without it, thus; the difference measures its effective utility;" such is the mental process by which individual or society makes a valuation. The three typical cases in our former illustration apply equally here. Would an article in possession, if removed, be replaced without sacrifice, like the air in a closed room? The measure of its effective utility is nothing. Would it be replaced at some sacrifice? Its effective utility is gauged by the sacrifice. Would an imperfect substitute take its place? Its utility is gauged by the two-fold sacrifice entailed. These cases are all; for there is nothing, not paintings by Raphael, nor gems from monarchs' diadems, for which some substitute, perfect or imperfect, is not to be had.

When society, as a consumer, has bought a thing, it must locate it in the organic whole. The locating process has its laws, and society must estimate what is offered to it in the market in view of the place in the social body which, by the laws of this higher physiology, it is compelled to fill. There are laws of property, fixed principles of distribution; these are facts to be recognized, conditions which determine the estimate which society is to make. As a molecule of nutriment in the human system does not diffuse itself through the body, but passes, by the circulating organs to the part that needs it, so useful commodities, molecules of social nutriment, unerringly follow the circulatory laws of the social system. Nerve tissue to the nerves, bone tissue to the bones, each particle reaches the place for which it is adapted.

It would be interesting, in itself, to analyze the process of distribution, and determine the forces which locate, in the social organism, the things which it buys for consumption. It would, however, extend this chapter unduly, and would lead us at once into detailed and analytical modes of study, which are foreign to our present purpose. It is sufficient, for the present, to notice that there are fixed laws of social circulation, and that whatever is taken from the market is located in, the social body, by laws which society is not at liberty to violate. It becomes evident, then, that a thing may have a fixed market value, while its value in use is indefinitely great or indefinitely small, according to its location. The poor man's loaf; what an intense desire it satisfies! As removed, its utility is measured by hunger; as replaced, by hard labor. The rich man's loaf; what a bagatelle in his estimation! Even its absence would but modify an abundant bill of fare, while its replacement would cost an inappreciable sacrifice. How values in use would be augmented could the location of articles be arbitrarily changed. Yet such a wholesale confiscation would mean the most violent of revolutions, and would lead to a chaotic condition fatal to the welfare of all. Yet better systems of social circulation may be before us, in the future, if we can but wait for their development.

The expression value in exchange has, for the sake of clearness, been, thus far, avoided; since, by its origin and common use, it is adapted to signify something different from either of the kinds of value which we have considered. It should mean simply indirect value in use, or the measure of the utility, to the owner of a thing, of the commodities which he can get in exchange for that thing in the market. It is as abstract as any form of value; it is not the things themselves which the person can get in exchange, but the measure of their utility to him. While completely distinct from market value, it is dependent on it; society's estimate of the utility of an article to itself determines what it will give for it, and what society gives, the individual seller receives.

The inaccuracy of the term purchasing power, often used as synonymous with value in exchange, consists mainly in its implying a power in the commodity itself to effect a purchase. Such power resides in men, not in things. If it be intended to indicate the quality in things that satisfies wants and influences men's actions, the name of that quality is utility. If it be intended to denote the degree to which it satisfies wants and influences action, the term is meas-

ure of utilty, or value. If what is meant be the rate
at which exchanges are made, in consequence of this
influence, a less misleading expression would be ratio
of exchange, or barter price. This is one of society's
two modes of expressing valuations; as its estimate of
utility expressed in terms of a conventional unit is
ordinary price, so that estimate expressed in general
comparisons is barter price.

It is not intended, just here, to make a treatise on
value; and the intricacies of this complicated theme
cannot be discussed, nor even alluded to. It would
be a source of satisfaction to apply the broad principles laid down to the more interesting of them. We
should learn, for example, the incorrectness of the
current doctrine of the absence of any real standard
of measurement for value. The standard exists,
though psychological in character and difficult of use.
Difference of subjective condition, measure of gratification, is the basis of the measurements of utility
which give value. The attempt to attain a unit for
such measurements will not lead us into the unprofitable intricacies which result from the theory that value
is fundamentally relative, based on mutual comparisons
in which A measures B, and B, A, and there is no
positive unit. Though too immaterial for accurate
use, the standard exists, and the aim should be to
recognize and approximate it.

The aim of this chapter is attained if, without

attempting to discuss intricate phenomena of value,
it has succeeded in truly stating the fundamental principles which govern them; if it has shown the nature
of value, as a measure of a quality of things, its
inseparable connection with utility, the nature of
utility, absolute and effective, and the part played by
society as an organic unit in valuing processes. After
this we are prepared for microscopy. Now we may
fix the attention on individuals, and their complicated
interactions. They will no longer confuse and lead
into mazes of logical wandering, but will throw the
same light on the general laws with which we start
that the curious movement of microscopic corpuscles
in the blood throw on the general movement of the
life-giving current. We should push the analysis to
greater lengths than is done by those current methods
of study whose fault is their minuteness. We should
study the very nature of man himself; for the ultimate
forces of society, as of physical nature, are atomic;
the individual is the originator and the end of every
movement. He is microcosmical, like the monad of
Leibnitz, a mirror of the universe; and the philosophy
of value and of other phenomena of society can be
grasped only by a view that is broad enough to
include the entire social organism, but, at the same
time, minute enough to apprehend the nature of the
social atom.

CHAPTER VI.

THE LAW OF DEMAND AND SUPPLY.

VALUE expresses itself in the quantitative ratio in which commodities exchange for each other in the market. This ratio is determined by Demand and Supply. It is not matter but utilities which are created by labor and destroyed by use, and which are, therefore, the subjects of Production and Consumption; they are, in like manner, the subjects of Exchange and Distribution.

A commodity is to be regarded as an aggregate of utilities held together by a common material basis. These qualities are of different kinds, and each appeals with a certain force to the desires of men. The strength of the desire for a commodity equals the aggregate strength of the desires for the various services which it can render.

Consumers gratify their wants in the order of their intensity, as far as their available means permit. A dry but useful formula will best define the demand with which political economy has to deal. Let A, B, C, D, and E represent different objects of desire; let the strength of the wants, in the case of a class of persons, vary in a scale from 5 to 1, that for A being the most

intense. Let the price of each be represented by a
single unit of value. The scale will stand as follows: —

A, B, C, D, E, = Different objects of desire.
5, 4, 3, 2, 1, = Relative intensity of desires.

The man with one unit of means available for present
use will purchase A ; the one with two units, A and B ;
the one with four units, A, B, C, and D. In each case
there will be a definite point where purchases will cease ;
and though an article which lies beyond that limit in
the scale could easily be purchased, it will not be so,
because of the mental attitude of the possible purchaser.
The man with three units of means will not buy D nor
E, though he might take them both and have a unit
left.

Demand for what falls within the purchase limit is
the "effectual demand" of the traditional theory. The
limit is determined by the price of the article, and the
available means and the mental status of purchasers.
The subjective factor last named is the most inconstant,
and produces the most sudden changes in the market.

Under a regime of free competition prices are adjusted by a simple law. If the supply of a particular
kind of commodity be regarded as fixed, as during brief
intervals it may be, it will be offered at a tentative price,
which will be subsequently raised or lowered until the
quantity offered is found to be within the purchase
limit of persons enough to take it. The tentative price

is, in many cases, too high; a part of the supply is then found to lie above the limit, and this, therefore, remains unsold. If there is a necessity for selling it, the price is gradually lowered, and each step of the decline brings the article within some one's purchase limit, and thus secures a new " effectual demander."

How far must the price fall in order to accomplish this enlargement of the market? The answer depends on the nature of the want to which the utilities embodied in the article appeal. The necessaries of life are the objects of a desire so intense and universal that it is habitually satisfied by nearly all members of a community. This want would stand at 5 in our ideal scale, and the man with but one unit of means would use it in procuring the articles which supply it. It is impossible to secure many new customers for the plainest kinds of food; no cheapness of provisions will induce more men to eat than already do so. To induce the present purchasers to consume more than they have heretofore done would be another method of enlarging the market; but the possibility of doing this is also limited. The want of mere food is inexpansive; a definite quantity completely satisfies it, and most persons secure about that quantity.

Wheat is not the plainest material for food, and the desire for it could not, with strict accuracy, be placed at the bottom of the scale; but it is near enough to that point to illustrate the principle. The desire for wheat

is intense, universal and inexpansive; a definite quantity is now purchased, and but little more is wanted.
This fact is the basis of the very disproportionate
fluctuations in its price which follow changes in the
supply. A large crop of wheat is worth far less in the
aggregate than a small one; and statistics have led Mr.
Tooke to the conclusion cited by Mr. Mill, that an
unrelieved deficit of one-third in the general corn crop
of England might advance the price tenfold.

With utilities which minister to wants midway in the
scale the case is different. These desires, as we have
seen, are indefinitely expansive, but decrease in intensity as the desired objects are supplied. This is true
of what may be termed the qualitative increments of
the necessaries of life. An improved variety may find
a market where an increased amount fails to do so.
The man who has food enough, such as it is, may easily
become a customer for something better. To leave the
quantity unchanged and improve the quality is to make
a net addition of a qualitative increment. It is to offer
for sale no new commodity, but a new utility of a higher
sort, one which ministers to wants lying midway in the
scale and comparatively expansive.

For this reason the natural growth of production
tends to take a qualitative direction, improving rather
than quantitatively increasing the food, clothing, furnishings, etc., of a community. Making no more shoes
than formerly, the shops of Lynn may, by making better

shoes, create many more utilities, and in this is afforded
an outlet for an indefinitely increased expenditure of
labor and capital. General over-production of qualitative increments is a theoretical and practical impossi-
bility; and the turning of productive energies in this
direction has resulted, in fact, in constantly raising the
standard of living of all classes. Whether the laboring
class has received its due proportion of benefit from this
cause is a question generally answered in the negative;
but of the fact of an absolute advance in the standard
of living of that class there is no doubt.

Wants of the highest grade are indefinitely expansive,
and increase in intensity with an increased supply of
the objects that gratify them. They are less universally developed than those of the lower grades; but
they have, in every man, at least a rudimentary existence, and are always strengthened by exercise. Cheap
books ensure reading, and thus an increased appetite
for reading. A fall in the general price of publications
ensures larger sales to habitual consumers, and increases
the number of the consuming class. The most expansive of all markets is that for the appliances for intellectual, æsthetic and moral growth. Here is a limitless
outlet for productive energy, and the extent to which
it is utilized is the gauge of genuine economic progress.

Accompanying the highest motives, and imitating
their action, here as elsewhere, is that love of esteem,
that universal and not unworthy vanity, already re-

ferred to. This motive creates a highly expansive market for whatever acts as a badge of social caste. Yet it is this identical want the working of which produces the most frequent and sudden fluctuations of value. It demands conformity to a changing style in clothing, furnishings, decorations, dwelling, equipage and an infinitude of semi-æsthetic form utilities.

The fluctuations in price resulting from this cause greatly over-balance, within limited intervals, those resulting from changes in supply. Fashion makes and destroys utilities capriciously and on a vast scale. The garment that is to-day as comfortable and as comely as it ever was, has lost over night the caste-marking power which is one of its major utilities, and its value is reduced by a half. Civilization multiplies the finer form utilities the value of which fashion dominates, and increases the importance of this changeful influence.

Under a regime of free competition most utilities have a normal price, toward which, during long intervals of time, the market rate continually tends. This normal price is that which will afford to the workmen engaged in the production ordinary wages, to the capitalist current interest, and to the employer an average profit. If the selling price is above this amount, there is an inducement to enlarged production, which reduces the current price to the normal limit. If, for any reason, the market yields less than a normal rate, there is a necessity for curtailed production, which raises the market price to the natural limit. During a long term of years utilities, as embodied in products, sell for the cost of production and an average profit.

Amid these changes in the quantity produced the cost of production does not remain stationary. The normal price is never, during a long interval, fixed. Certain commodities, when created in increased amount, have been said to require a more than proportionate increase of labor. To double the present wheat supply would, according to the current theory, involve more than double the present expenditure in production. The law of "diminishing returns" of agriculture becomes, in terms of the formulas here employed, a law of increasing costliness of elementary utilities. It means, not that food will be scarce and men hungry, when the world is more densely peopled, but that the food supply, enlarged as it must and will be, will cost more labor per capita than at present.

The basis of this accepted principle is the fact that elementary utilities are created through the action of the vital forces of the soil, and that nature is not everywhere equally generous. The best land is used first, and afterwards that which rewards labor less liberally. The normal price of that which man wins from unequally liberal nature must rise as the growth of population occasions an enlarged demand for food, and as this, in turn, compels a resort to poorer and poorer soils. More and more in the sweat of his face must man eat his

bread, though he may procure comforts and intellectual
enjoyments with a constantly lessening effort.

It is conceded that the invention of machines, and the
adoption of improved processes in agriculture retard the
operation of the law of diminishing returns, and hold it,
during considerable intervals, completely in abeyance.
It is conceded that improved means of transportation
have a similar effect. Had the American continent, in
Ricardo's time, been towed bodily across the Atlantic,
and anchored with its shores in contact with the British
Islands, the wheat fields of Dakota would not have been
as near to London, if distance be estimated in cost of
transportation, as they are to-day. Many a mill, a half-
century ago, revolved its wooden wheel in parts of
England from which the grist could by no means then
known be carried to London with so small a deduction
for expenses by the way as can the present output of
the mills of Minnesota. The relief thus experienced
by the consumers of flour in London is as real as though
wheat-raising in England had become more remunera-
tive. Wheat, in the London market, is an aggregate of
elementary and place utilities, and improved facilities
of transportation have so cheapened the latter as to
counterbalance the increased costliness of the former.

A counteracting influence, to which little justice is
done, is that of the accumulation of capital and the
reduction of interest. The expenditure of capital
enough will make the best of land out of what now

ranks as the poorest; and if that capital will but content itself with a sufficiently small proportion of the returns of cultivation, the reward of the labor itself may be as large as that now realized from the soils in use. When a hundred million dollars are available for dredging the deposit from the mouth of the Mississippi, and depositing it on the sands of Florida, for a return of one per cent upon the investment, it is conceivable that labor may win as much from the use of the artificially made land as it does from that which is not burdened by the claims of the capitalist.

It may be maintained that all these influences are temporary; that the principle at the basis of the law of the diminishing returns of agriculture is permanent; and that, in the end, this tendency must overcome the others. The time may be remote, but it is said to be coming, when labor applied to the soil must create a smaller product than now rewards it, and when man must win by harder and harder effort the privilege of mere existence. It remains, therefore, to notice an influence which is a chief basis of economic optimism, since it is capable of holding the law of diminishing returns for an indefinite period in abeyance.

We do not here combat that essential Malthusianism which maintains that a retarding of the rate of increase of population is an ultimate necessity, if humanity is to fully enjoy the earth, and to perfect itself. The probable condition of the future is that of a constantly increasing population, and of a constantly diminishing rate of increase. These tendencies, acting together, would give, at some point in the indefinite future, a comparatively stationary condition, in which population, having become exceedingly dense, would show, from decade to decade, little, if any, increase. Malthusianism of a certain type would predict a reign of increasing misery during the indefinitely long period before the stationary condition is realized. Is there ground for such a belief in economic law?

The cost of creating form utilities is constantly lessening; and form utilities are more and more preponderating in the wealth of society. That which humanity, as a whole, enjoys costs it a continually lessening sacrifice.

That which produces form utilities is not the creative power of nature, but the transforming power of men; and this power becomes progressively efficient as production enlarges. New motive powers, machines, and processes are multiplying, and promise to increase, beyond any discernible limit, the capacity of man to transform what nature places in his hand. If elementary utilities become costlier by one-quarter, and form utilities cheaper by one-half, the resultant is a gain for humanity in the enjoyments which it can secure.

A numerical illustration will place this principle in a

clear light. Let us suppose that the influences which
retard the action of the principle of diminishing returns in agriculture have done their full work, and
that the law is asserting itself, and causing a day's
subsistence for society to cost, decade after decade, an
increasing proportion of the day's labor. Let us say
that, in the year 2000, two-fifths of the labor of society, as a producing organism, is expended in creating
elementary utilities, and three-fifths in creating form
and place utilities. Let us suppose that the lapse of
a century reverses this numerical proportion, causing
three-fifths of the total labor to be expended upon the
elementary utilities; does it follow that society gets,
in the aggregate, less than before for the total effort
of a day or a year? Not if the labor expended upon
form and place utilities has gained in efficiency more
than other labor has lost. If the social effort, which
is still available for the creation of the higher utilities, has become twice as effective as before, then the
total labor of the producing organism will secure for
it a far greater aggregate result. Mankind may be indefinitely better off, on the whole, when three-fifths of
its total effort is crudely agricultural. If it takes account of stock at the end of a year, estimates its total
gains and sacrifices, and compares them with those recorded for a similar period a century before, it will
find this as a result: it has been fed, as during the
earlier year, and it has been better served in every

other direction. The two-fifths of its labor force, still available for the creation of higher utilities, has fashioned its clothing and built its dwellings in a better manner; and it has instructed, amused, and, in æsthetic and spiritual ways, ministered to it far better than was possible in the days when a larger but less efficient force was expended in these directions. In the terms of our formulas, the utilizations of society have increased, and the organism has approached nearer to its economic goal. Its intelligence has triumphed over resisting nature, and, though she succeeds in exacting a larger and larger proportionate effort in the production of crude subsistence, she undergoes from decade to decade a more complete subjugation. She is compelled to minister more and more subserviently to the higher wants of man.

The law of diminishing returns in agriculture would, in itself, give promise of a condition in the future in which food will be as plentiful as now, but in which the gaining of it will absorb an increased proportion of the labor of the social organism. The effect of this would be to lessen the amount of labor available for the creation of finer products, and this diminution would be far more than compensated by the greater effectiveness of this labor. We may, then, admit the law of diminishing returns in agriculture, and fear nothing for the future of humanity. The basis of economic welfare is broadening, and if this tendency

is ever reversed, it will be at a time too far in the
future to be a subject of present consideration.

The inaccuracies of thought in the orthodox theory
of Demand and Supply are chiefly of importance for
their bearing on the outlook for the future of the race.
It will be remembered that Mr. Mill's statement of the
law divides commodities into three classes, namely,
those which cannot be reproduced, those which can be
produced in any quantity at a uniform cost, and those
which can be produced in enlarged quantity, but only
at an increasing cost. Articles of the first class are said
to have no normal or "natural" price; those of the second have a natural price which is uniform, regardless
of the quantity produced; and those of the third have
a natural price which rises with increasing production.
For commodities the cost of which diminishes with increasing production the theory makes no provision, and
the omission is unfortunate.

If the law of Demand and Supply be based on what
labor creates, not matter but its utilities, it will be seen
that the first class named in the traditional statement
of the theory can scarcely be said to exist. To reproduce an article is to reproduce its serviceable qualities;
and it is, perhaps, never the case that an article is offered for sale of which none of the utilities can be
thus duplicated. Where any of the major utilities of
a commodity can be reproduced, the article is, in so
far, subjected to the ordinary laws of the market, and

its price is, in part, determined by the cost of reproduction of those particular utilities.

It is obvious, without careful analysis, that the price
of rare articles is greatly influenced by the possibility
of producing substitutes for them. To multiply approximate reproductions of a rare painting is to lessen
the intensity of the competition for the painting
itself. A Cremona violin of a given age sells for less
than it would command if other violins of nearly
equal quality could not be manufactured. The price
of the rare instrument consists of two distinguishable
parts, first, the market price of fine violins, as governed by the cost of production, and, secondly, a
special premium for the unique excellence of the old
instrument.

Accurately stated, the law is this: a few commodities
contain certain utilities which cannot be duplicated,
and others which can be so; the former command a
price determined by the direct action of demand and
supply, and the latter tend to sell at a normal rate,
fixed by the cost of reproduction. The market price of
such commodities is the aggregate price of their different utilities. Mr. Mill's own illustrations prove this
principle. Rare wines contain properties peculiar to
themselves, and others which are common to a wide
range of similar products. The value of the Johannis-
berger vintage consists of the market value of an equal
quantity of other fine wine, plus a premium for its own

inimitable flavor. The price of antique statues, when they fall into the market, is somewhat affected by the value of substitutes which may be multiplied at will; and the same is true of all the articles enumerated.

If there are commodities of which the supply may be increased indefinitely at a uniform rate of cost, it is because the cheapening of the form utilities embodied in them chances to exactly counterbalance the growing costliness of the elementary. A fine watch consists mainly of elementary utilities, in the case, and of form utilities, in the movement. If the consumption of watches were to be quadrupled, it might happen that the greater costliness of the one part would offset the greater cheapness of the other. The second of the traditional classes may have a fortuitous and transient existence.

The third class has a somewhat better basis. If the law of diminishing returns in agriculture were admitted, it would be necessary to accept the conclusion that crude nutriment will become costlier as population increases. It would then be of importance to note that there is a class not noticed in the traditional theory in the case of which the reverse of the above law is true. Commodities consisting mainly of form utilities are unquestionably becoming cheaper; and among these are all products which minister to intellectual, æsthetic and spiritual wants. If the conditions of the future were to involve plainer living, they would at least be more favorable to high thinking; and we might welcome a tendency which would make it necessary for men to forego some of the sensuous enjoyments of life, if it, at the same time, enriched them in intelligence, refinement and moral character. If the man of the future is to be wiser and better than the man of to-day, we need not be troubled with the question whether he will or will not be ·happier. We do not admit, however, that the spiritual gain is to be purchased by a physical sacrifice. The world is, in fact, becoming more tolerable to man as an animal, and it is becoming indefinitely more favorable to him as a rational being.

CHAPTER VII.

THE LAW OF DISTRIBUTION.

THAT mankind as a whole shall become richer does not, of necessity, involve an increase of human welfare. That is dependent, not only on the quantity of wealth accumulated, but on the mode in which it is shared. A better division of the results of industry might atone for some diminution in the amount produced. As bearing on the prospects of mankind, there are three practical problems to be solved; of these the first is how to create, with the least sacrifice, the largest aggregate of utilities; the second is how to justly divide the gain; and the third is how to ensure in the product that quality which shall cause it to minister to permanent rather than to transient well-being. We are now to consider the second of these problems. The quantity of wealth created is, in fact, increasing faster than population; are the equities of distribution also increasing?

The mode of dividing the proceeds of social industry is changing, under our eyes, at a rate so rapid that it is difficult for a scientific system to keep pace with it. Demand and supply are the regular agents of distribution, and have divided the stream of social

production into three channels, containing respectively
Rent, Gross Profits, and Wages. Of these, the first
has been traditionally regarded as determined by a
more or less independent law, and it will be conven-
ient for our purposes to accept this theory, and confine our attention to the division which determines
the amount of wages and of profits.

Vital as are the interests centering in the law of
wages, the subject is full of unsettled theoretical
questions of a kind that, as one would suppose, ought
to be forever decided by a little clear and candid
thought. There is, moreover, a moral element in
these questions. Points of fact suggest problems in
equity. What are wages? From what source do
they come? What determines their amount? These
questions suggest the inquiry whether, in nature,
source, and amount, they are what they ought to be,
or whether there is, in the present transactions of
class with class, a series of wrongs which demand a
reform, and, as an alternative, threaten a revolution.

In the absence of a scientific answer to the points
of equity at issue, and of one so clearly proven as to
compel belief, interest dictates the replies given in
the greater number of cases; and this fact arrays one
social class against another, and makes it possible for
each to claim a moral basis for its action. The contests of interest between capitalists and laborers are
intensified by counter-claims in equity; and the prob-

lem thrust upon society is not merely how to divide a sum, but how to adjust rights and obligations.

Politics cannot escape the dominant influence of these ethico-economic issues. The solidarity of capital on the one hand, and of labor on the other, are things of which the founders of our republic thought as little as the founders of our system of economics. The strain to which this influence is about to subject our institutions would be indefinitely less if the counterclaims in equity could be in so far settled that men not biased by belligerent feeling might be in substantial agreement concerning them. If it is humanly possible to thus settle the questions at the basis of the law of wages, no scientific work can be more immediately and widely beneficent. These questions tend, if rightly answered, to public order; if wrongly answered, to communism; and, if unanswered, to agitation and peril.

The very allusions to the solidarity of labor and of capital which it has been necessary to make, may seem to have placed out of order any farther discussion of the accepted law of demand and supply. That has been supposed to rest on the antecedent fact of free competition, to which solidarity is the antithesis. If labor, on the one hand, and capital, on the other, should ever act as units in the dividing of the product of their industrial action, true competition would be totally suppressed. Such a condition is one impossible extreme, while the other is the condition of unhindered competition which crude thinking has placed at the basis of economic law. The facts of actual industry are between the extremes, and a theory of Distribution must conform to the facts.

Free competition itself is, as we shall later see, not an unrestricted scramble for gain. Of these two processes the former has recently existed, and in certain fields still exists, while the latter is so completely antiquated that the most we have to do with it is to show its monstrosity. The only possible mode of attaining a true law of distribution is to ascertain how demand and supply would operate under a regime of competition in the true sense free, and, secondly, how that action is modified by the growth of what, in the absence of an authorized term, I should like to call *solidarism*, or the tendency of both labor and capital to aggregate, and act, within extensive fields, as units. There is, indeed, no prospect that competition will ever be totally suppressed; in spite of all encroachments on its territory it will doubtless have a residual field of action in permanent possession.

Nothing is more confusing than the view which rep-resents demand and supply as acting promiscuously on everything bought and sold. This view implies a general receptacle termed a market, into which commodities are indiscriminately thrown, and in which, in some way, they receive a valuation. In this theory of the market and its action labor is usually classed as a commodity, the price of which is fixed in the same manner as that of other articles in the promiscuous assortment.

The action of demand and supply is systematic and capable of clear analysis. It proceeds in one way in the case of products ready for social consumption, in another in the case of the specific utilities which workers in the producing series impart, and in still another in the case of the shares of capitalists and laborers who jointly create a particular utility. To fix the value of clothing ready for use is one thing; to divide that value among agriculturists, transporters, manufacturers and tailors, is another; and to adjust the proportions falling to capitalists and to laborers in each of these producing groups is still another. The entire distributing process consists of a division, a sub-division and a farther subdivision of the general product of social industry. Demand and supply have a primary, a secondary and a tertiary field of action.

Social production takes place, as already noticed, not by a single operation, but by a succession of many. One producing agency begins with crude nature, and so modifies it as but partially to prepare it for rendering its service to men; another and another continue the operation. The ultimate result of the action of all is a completed product, and the particular change effected by each may be distinguished as a sub-product. The elementary utility created by mining is the first sub-product of a certain series; the place utility imparted by transportation is a second; the form utility resulting from smelting is a third; that from puddling and rolling is a fourth; that from cutting is a fifth; while the aggregate of all is the keg of nails of our former illustration.

In the order of production the series stands as follows: —

SYNTHESIS RESULTING IN THE COMPLETED PRODUCT, NAILS.

1st Sub-Product. Elementary Utility. Ore.	2d Sub-P. Place U. Transporta'n.	3d Sub-P. Form U. Smelting.	4th Sub-P. Form U. Puddling, etc.	5th Sub-P. Form U. Cutting.
Resulting from the joint action of Capital and Labor.	Joint result of C'' and L'.	Joint result of C'' and L''.	Joint result of C''' and L'''.	Joint result of C'''' and L''''.

The first sub-product is an elementary utility created by capital and labor; the second is a place utility created by another kind of capital and labor; the third, fourth and fifth are specific form utilities, each created by its own variety of capital and labor. The complete product, nails, is the outcome of the application of C, C', C'', C''' and C'''', and of L, L', L'', L''' and L''''; it is the resultant of five specific kinds of effort, each assisted by the form of capital adapted to it. Social production is, thus, a synthesis of clearly distinguishable elements.

Distribution is the reverse of this synthesis; it is an analytical process which resolves the above aggregate into its components. It deals, however, with pure quantity; it separates, not commodities into their component utilities, but values into a series of quantitative increments. It determines the amount of social wealth embodied in a quantity of nails; it then fixes the proportion of that sum represented by each of the sub-products which constitute the nails, and, again, the proportion of each of these latter amounts which belongs to capital and to labor. In terms of our diagram, distribution determines the value of the Completed Product, resolves that amount into the values of 1st sub-P. 2d sub-P. etc., and then subdivides the value of 1st sub-P. between C and L, that of 2d sub-P. between C′ and L′, etc.

The steps of the actual distribution follow, in time, the order of production, which is the reverse of the logical order of division. The secondary subdivision is made, in reality, first. The first sub-product is distributed among capitalists and laborers before the amount of that sub-product is fixed by an actual sale. The mining company must usually pay its men before actually parting with its ore. It proceeds thus with but little risk, since the value of the ore is sufficiently gauged by current sales by other ore producers. In like manner the value of the sub-products is, in each case, determined before that of the completed product is actually fixed by a final sale. Ore, pig iron, bar iron, etc., are sold before the particular nails which embody the value of all are placed upon the market. The value of the nails is, in the meanwhile, sufficiently gauged by other sales of that commodity.

The final sale of the completed product is, in reality, a dividing process. It is a quantitative division of the general product of the industrial organism. That which fixes the purchasing power of nails assigns to the nail-producing group its quantitative proportion of the total utilities resulting from industry. Society is here to be regarded as the purchaser; the sellers are the creators of the last sub-product in the series; and the parties in the division effected by the sale are the nail-producing group, on the one hand, and all other groups, on the other. The fate of the whole group is thus, in a sense, intrusted to the creators of the last utility in the series, who, by the nature of the arrangement, must act as selling agents.

The earlier sub-producers have received their aggregate share of the product by the sale of bar iron to the nail-cutters; the still earlier ones have obtained theirs in the sale of pig iron, etc. Each of the earlier sales in the series effects a division between the groups of producers whose work has preceded the sale, and those whose work is to follow it.

The reward of each particular producing group is determined by the buying of the antecedent sub-products, and the subsequent selling of them with the addition of another utility. The nail-maker buys material, transforms and sells it ; and his product, quantitatively considered, is the difference in the measure of the utility of the article, which is caused by the transformation. He converts that value into currency by buying bars and selling nails.

The process which divides a sub-product, quantitatively considered, between capitalists and laborers differs in principle from the more general divisions, and demands fuller consideration. In the meanwhile we need to examine the mode in which demand and supply operate, as adjusting agents, in affecting the primary and secondary divisions. Let us, for simplicity, take an ideal case, and make a tabular representation of the conditions presented. Let an insular society, disconnected from the commercial world, be supposed to contain a thousand wool-growers, twenty wool-buyers, fifty manufacturers of woolen goods, and five hundred merchant-tailors. The series may be represented as follows : —

500 Tailors, and Employés.
50 Manufacturers, and Operatives.
20 Wool-buyers, and Assistants.
1000 Wool-growers, and Employés.

The total product of the labor of all is the clothing of the men of the island. The society contains many other groups, each having, as the result of its industry, a particular product, sufficient, in quantity, for the

wants of all inhabitants. The conditions are, of course,
simplified out of all detailed resemblance to the facts of
life, and yet present, with the greater clearness, the one
great fact of actual social economy which crude thinking disregards, to its utter confusion, that, namely, of
certain necessary and permanent limits of competitive
action. The formal modification of the above table
which, in a completer discussion, it would be most necessary to make, is that which would express the relation
of producers of the cruder materials to several groups
of producers of the finer utilities. One man may belong to several such groups as those in our table. A
farmer may raise corn as well as keep sheep, and may
thus be a member of the group which feeds the insular
community, as well as to that which clothes it. He
works in two capacities and receives a specific reward
in each. In like manner the wool-buyer may sell his
product to carpet-makers, as well as to makers of cloth,
and so belong, in so far as a part of his effort is concerned, to a group which provides a variety of house
furnishings. The horizontal lines including classes of
sub-producers need, for a nearer resemblance to the
complex system of social industry, to be prolonged
through other general groups. This complication may
be studied at will; it does not affect one primarily
important conclusion to which a study of the simpler
grouping would lead us, namely, that all true competition is between similar sub-producers. Resolving the

complex process popularly termed competition into the
elements of which, in an earlier chapter, we have found
that it is composed, we now see that the part which is
truly competitive, the rivalry in under-selling, is confined, in every case, between two adjacent horizontal
lines; while the bargaining process takes place across a
line. The fifty manufacturers compete only with each
other; they buy across the line which separates them
from wool-dealers, and sell across that which separates
them from tailors.

The group which makes clothing for our ideal society contains 1,570 specific producing agencies, each
having its employés. Wool-growers and wool-buyers
have some hired men; manufacturers have many, and
tailors have their necessary quota. There may be
15,000 capitalists and laborers in the general group
which produces the clothing of a hundred thousand
persons. If the groups were completely distinct, and if
the consumption of clothing were *per capita*, eighty-
five per cent of the product of this group would be a
surplus.

It is a matter of course that the disposable part
of the product of this group must, in the general
exchanges of society, purchase what its members use
of the surplus products of all other groups. Our
15,000 persons get food, dwellings, furnishings, books,
etc., by selling all the clothing which they do not
use; and every other group acts in like manner. This

is one primary fact in distribution; but, in itself, it
fixes the price of no specific product in terms of any
other.

It will be remembered that, in the traditional economic science, this principle that surplusses offset each
other, has been applied to international trade. With
certain allowances for debts, exports pay for imports;
and this fact is of importance as bearing on the movements of currency. Yet, as affecting the distribution
of wealth, national lines are not of primary consequence. With due allowance for debts and taxes,
it is true of any local division whatever that what
goes out of it pays for what comes into it. This is
true of a county, a township, or a farm; that which
crosses the boundary of either one of these divisions in
an outward direction pays for what crosses it in an
inward direction. This fact would be worth mentioning if counties, townships, and farms coined money,
and troubled themselves about the balance of trade;
in discussing the distribution of wealth, it is not worth
mentioning. The outcome of the industry of the world
is not divided among states, counties, townships, and
farms; but among producing groups and sub-groups,
and then among the capitalists and laborers in each.

Competition follows necessarily and permanently the
lines indicated in our diagram. These demarcations
are made by the nature of the functions of the groups
thus described. These non-competing groups are

totally distinct from those discussed by Professor
Cairnes, which are based on the personal qualities of
laborers. Of these we shall speak later; their importance in the process of distribution lies in the fact
that a laborer cannot easily transfer himself from one
class to another. In the grouping represented in our
diagram we take no account of *personnel*. For aught
that we now know or care, men may pass from group
to group, — and from generation to generation it is
certain that the membership must change, — yet,
through all personal changes the group itself continues
a distinct thing, separated from every other by the
nature of its function.

It is true, in practice, that migration from group to
group is not altogether easy, and this fact bears, in
a manner later to be considered, on the law of wages;
yet, while a man is in a particular group, the limits
of the competition in which he takes part are fixed
by this fact. The nail-maker of to-day can compete
only with nail-makers; and though he were able to
become a tailor to-morrow, he would, in the new position, find equally sharp boundaries drawn about his
competitive action.

The primary field in which the rivalry in under-
selling takes place is in the sale of completed products
to society; the secondary field is in the sale of the
sub-products to classes in the producing groups; and
the ternary field is in the transactions which adjust
wages and profits within the sub-groups.

In each of these provinces of action there may exist
three more or less distinct conditions in respect to
competition. There may be, first, the conservative
competition in which economists of a few years ago
were able to see realized a general harmony of social
interests. There may be, secondly, the fiercer contest
in which eventual success comes to a participant
through the extermination of rivals, the process well
named "cut-throat" competition. There may be,
thirdly, a combination of parties in the strife, which
produces a monopoly, tempered, as we shall hereafter
see, by a certain latent competition. The first two
conditions would seem to shade into one another by
easy gradations, while the second and the third would
appear to be the antitheses of each other. The competitive struggle might, seemingly, progress in fierce-
ness from a rivalry conducted on a live-and-let-live
principle to a war of extermination; while between
such a war and the combination which excludes all
strife there would appear to be nothing in common.
Yet the first process is the result of a distinct set of
industrial conditions, while the second and third are
the product of another set. Easy and tolerant competition is the antithesis of monopoly; the cut-throat
process is the father of it.

At the time when economic science was in process
of formulating, the functions of manufacturer and of
merchant were merged in a large number of produc-

tive groups. The word "shop," as signifying a place
for retail dealing, is, in itself, a record of a comparatively primitive, industrial system in which manufactures were conducted in a multitude of little shops,
whose owners often retailed their products. Large
remnants of this system exist in every European country; but in America it is a thing of the past.

The era of manufacturing by hand for local con-
stituencies was an era of conservative competition.
Custom played here the part ascribed to it by Mr.
Mill, as a restraining agency in the struggle; but that
custom itself had a basis in a moral sentiment, and in
the conditions of traffic which afforded to this moral
force a free field of action.

In retail dealing, even in our own time and country,
competition is far more conservative than in most
industrial fields; yet the pressure in the direction of
destructive competition in this department is indefinitely stronger than before the general introduction
of machinery into manufactures. It is only large sales
that can atone for small profits; and the artizan retailer
of former times was debarred in two ways from securing such sales by means of a reduction in prices. He
could less easily increase his product than a modern
retailer can do; and, secondly, though he were to
increase the amount produced, he had no assurance
of increasing the quantity which he might sell. An
increase in the product of the little shop involved

more laborers and larger capital. The spirit of the time regarded with distrust an attempt of one dealer to injure his rivals by selling for less than a normal profit. The "good will" of a business was then no misnomer, but signified the personal confidence and kindly feeling existing between a dealer and his local constituency. He, perhaps, lived and worked where his ancestors had lived and worked before him, and appeared to inherit a prescriptive right to his customers' patronage.

The conservative competition in the sale of finished products to society transmitted itself through the industrial groups, and produced an equally tolerant relation among rival sub-producers. The man who sold material to the small artificer was, like his patron, debarred from great increase in production, and from great opportunity for large sales. Custom, based on good will and a sense of prescriptive right, governed, to a large extent, the sales which took place across the horizontal lines separating one producing class from another, and made the entire action of competition, in its primary and secondary fields, moderate and tolerant. The era was one of uneconomical methods of work, of divided and localized production, of large profits and small sales, of high prices to society as a consumer, of little general wealth, but of comparative equality and contentment among the middle class in the community.

What these conditions involved for the working class

we shall later see; in the meanwhile we need to notice the change in the action of competition, in its primary and secondary fields, which resulted from the introduction of machinery and the factory system. The conservative influences in the market for completed products were largely thrust aside by the changes following the use of steam, and a revolution took place in each of three distinct spheres, namely, in working processes, in class relations, and in the ethics of the market.

The first effect of the industrial change was the extermination of the general class of artisan retailers. The survivors of the guild-brethren whose shuttles wrought all fine fabrics for our ancestors are now crowded into a few fields where hand work is prized for its own sake. The utility of hand-worked laces and embroideries, as badges of social caste, still insures their production on a limited scale. Handicraftsmen hold, mainly under the protection of fashion, a few other fields in precarious tenure.

The method by which the machine has, in many cases, displaced the artisan has been by appealing to his own interest as a retailer; it is by offering to him, in his capacity of shopkeeper, goods for less than they would cost him as an artificer. The machine, the enemy of the tradesman in one of his capacities, is his friend in another. An illustration of this process may still occasionally be seen. The making of harnesses is not a process in which factory work has a relatively large advantage, and the local tradesman may still make and retail them; yet he can usually buy them for less than it costs him to manufacture them, and, except where an extra price is obtainable, on the ground of durability, he is compelled by self-interest to allow his own work to be driven from the field.

The mere retailer is able easily to increase his product; and, in increasing, he cheapens it, by the principle which accords the larger trade discount to the larger purchaser. If he can but increase his sales, he may lower his prices, to the extent of his larger discounts, without decreasing his rate of profit; but he may also decrease his percentage of profit without diminution of his absolute gains. Large purchases lower the cost of goods, and large sales more than atone for a smaller percentage of profit. Can the large sales be secured? Does the factory system change the attitude of a local constituency towards a retailer?

It is the man who makes a commodity, rather than the man who buys and sells it, who appears to a community to have a prescriptive right to patronage; and the strong sentiment of good will, which protected the artisan in his shop does not protect the retailer, who appears, to popular eye, to be a middle-man intercepting the profits of others. Mere interest comes more and more to determine where the public will buy its goods, and this fact gives a farther impetus to competition in the retail traffic.   This transmits itself in intensified form to the lower sub-groups in the series.   The retailer, under pressure of competition from men of his own class, has no choice but to buy where he can buy the cheapest, and competition of the most intense kind arises at the very point where, by the old system of local manufacture, it was excluded, namely, in the transactions between the maker and the vendor of commodities.   Rapid centralization follows this intense competition; productive establishments become few, large and ready for the next transition, that, namely, to a regime of association and monopoly.   The changes in working methods that must follow the use of steam were dimly foreseen by early inventors; the ulterior effects of it are not yet appreciated.   The revolution which was brewing in Watt's tea-kettle was threefold, affecting the structure of society and the moral nature of man.

NOTE. — There is, of course, a serious incompleteness in any discussion of Distribution which does not consider the Law of Rent. The products of which we have spoken, as divided between capitalists and laborers, must, if the traditional theory of rent be tacitly accepted, be regarded as consisting of what remains to the producing classes after rent has been paid.   The traditional theory enables us to take this view; it teaches that rent is the first deduction made from the gross returns of industry, and that it is determined, in amount, by an independent law.   This is not my real reason for omitting the discussion of it.   The Ricardian Law of Rent appears to me to require an extensive supplementing, which, for the purposes of the present work, it is better not to attempt.

CHAPTER VIII.

CERTAIN opponents of Mr. Henry George have committed the strategic error of attacking his system at an impregnable point, namely, his theory of the origin of wages. In the third chapter of "Progress and Poverty" he has proved that they come, not from capital, but from products. He has, indeed, fallen into an error greater than that which he refutes, in ignoring the productive action of capital. The product of which he speaks is that of "labor" alone; the employer takes the whole of it, returns a part as wages, and lives on the proceeds of a quasi-fraud. Of capital as a joint producer, and of the consequent claims of the man who owns and uses it, the theory takes no due account. On the single point, however, that products are the source from which the laborer derives his maintenance, Mr. George's reasoning is as conclusive as anything in mathematics.

The Wage-Fund doctrine once prevalent maintained that the laborer's pay comes from a portion of capital antecedently set apart for that purpose. Some influence, the nature of which has not been clearly analyzed, has predetermined that the whole of this fund

shall be used in wage payments. If the number of
laborers be constant, the rate of wages must vary
directly as the size of the fund. If the fund be constant, the rate of wages must vary inversely as the
number of laborers. The problem resolves itself into
a simple question of arithmetical division. Though
this crude form of the doctrine may be antiquated,
there are still many writers who retain so much of
it as to argue vigorously that wages are paid from a
fund of capital antecedently accumulated.

The key to the problem lies in the distinction between a wage payment regarded as a value, a thing
of pure quantity, and a wage payment regarded as a
mass of concrete commodities of a kind adapted to
the laborer's use. It is one thing to determine from
what sum the amount of wealth represented by wages
is deducted, and quite a different thing to ascertain
how that abstract quantity comes to embody itself
in bread, meat, clothing, implements, etc. If the
laborer can get the value which he requires for his
services, he can embody it in the necessary forms by
a process of exchange. As a problem in distribution
the present inquiry is, What is the real source of the
value which rewards the laborer?

Labor adds to the wealth of its employer. The
addition is necessary and continuous; from the moment when the mill begins to run to the moment
when it stops, labor, assisted by capital in different

forms, is increasing the possessions of the man or the company that employs it. Let the wheel of the engine make a dozen revolutions; there is an inch more of cloth upon every loom. The employer recognizes this addition to his assets, and would not fail to take account of it if he were making an accurate inventory. All through the day and the week the sum of his wealth is growing; and when he pays his men on Saturday night, he takes the amount of their wages, if pure quantity alone be considered, from the value that has come into existence during the working days.

Let a man pump water into a full tank, and get what he wants for use from the overflow; does the water for consumption come from the tank or from the pump? In a sense from both; and if important interests were dependent on the answer given, there would be here an opportunity for a fierce logomachy like that which has actually arisen over the origin of wages. The particular drops which are used come immediately from the tank; but the amount in it is undiminished, and the draught virtually comes from the supply furnished by the pump. Moreover, the size of the tank has no influence on the amount of the overflow; that is gauged by the volume of the inflowing stream. In like manner wages are taken immediately from a reservoir of capital; but the amount in that reservoir is undiminished, since the quantity which is drawn from it has already been added to it by the stream of products resulting from industry. It is the volume of products which sets limits to the amount of wages.

The hydraulic figure will, perhaps, bear straining to the extent of representing one other fact in the relation of capital to wages. If the water which overflows from the tank be regarded as better in quality than that which is pumped into it, if, for example, it loses its sediment by standing, the service rendered by the reservoir corresponds to a certain useful office performed by capital. The quality of what the workman receives is of importance to him, as well as its quantity. It needs to come to him in available forms. "The ploughman cannot eat the furrow," says Mr. George, though the furrow is wealth, and a share of it is wages, in the sense in which the term is used in Distribution. The weaver cannot eat the cloth upon the loom, nor can he even wear it. He must exchange it, or the employer must do so for him. Society must take it, and return bread, clothing, etc. This exchange demands social capital; it would be interesting to inquire how much, but the inquiry would take us into another department of economic science. It is safe to assert, without waiting for a full demonstration, that society does not lack the capital that is requisite for the purpose, and that wages are not kept down by any lack of means of exchanging them as the needs of the laborer may require.

Wages, in the primary sense of the term, are the workman's share in the value created by the industry in which he participates. They are a quantity of wealth, as determined by a process in Distribution. In a secondary sense they are that abstract value as embodied in available forms by a process in Exchange.

There is, then, a question of division at issue between the workmen and their employers. That division may be regarded in general or in detail; wages as a whole and profits as a whole come from a certain aggregate sum; the wages of particular groups of workmen and the profits of their employers come from distinguishable portions of that aggregate. The reward of the working class as a whole comes from the total value of the completed products of society; that of particular workmen and groups of workmen comes from the value of specific sub-products. In terms of our diagram the amount falling to L, L', L'', etc., taken as a whole, comes from the value of the product, nails; while the share of L comes from 1st Sub-P., that of L' from 2d Sub-P., etc. The wage in a particular case is determined, first, by the amount of the sub-product from which it is taken, and secondly, by the terms of the division between C and L. Assign fixed proportions of the sub-product to capital and to labor respectively, and the reward of each will vary directly as the sub-product. This would be the case in a system of coöperation, or in one of profit-

sharing of a certain kind. Let the sub-product be a
constant quantity, and wages and profits will vary
according to the division between them.

The historical fact of the past three hundred and
fifty years has been that real wages have declined for
three centuries and advanced for a half-century. The
decline was not continuous; there was a rapid fall, a
partial recovery, and a second fall, leaving the workmen, in other than specially favored countries, in
extreme wretchedness. This great decline in wages
took place during an era of generally conservative
competition; while the advance which has followed
it has been recent, and has taken place in an era
in which the money-getting spirit has overcome the
former conservative influences, and in which competition, in the fields in which it survives, has been
of an unsparing character. Both of the determining
causes above mentioned have contributed to this
result. There has been a vast increase in the quantity of wealth produced; and this fact may have sufficed to increase the laborer's reward without any
enlargement of his proportionate share of the sub-
product. Whether the division is, at the present day,
taking place on terms more favorable to the laborer
than those which ruled fifty years ago is of far less
consequence than the question whether the present
principle of division is one which must yield permanently better results than the old one. That real

wages are high this year is of little importance in comparison with the fact that they are adjusted by a process which promises to make them higher next year, and still higher in the years following, a process which offers a permanent guaranty against the resumption of the hopeless downward tendency which, under the former system, was regarded as "natural."

The old principle of division rendered gross injustice inevitable; the present principle makes equity possible. A fair bargain demands either a desire for justice on the part of the participants, or strategic equality between them. The weak and the powerful may deal equitably with each other if justice rather than selfish interests be the end in view; in the absence of this moral force weakness must be matched against weakness, and strength against strength. A maximum of justice in distribution is attained where the brute forces are evenly matched, and where moral influences are efficient. A minimum of justice results where brute forces are unequal, and moral forces wanting.

The phenomenon of the long era of declining wages was the concurrence of strategic inequality between capitalists and laborers, with a certain disorganization of the moral forces of society. The crude forces of capital and labor were not as unequal as they might have been, and moral forces were not utterly wanting. The general ethics of the market may have been bet-

ter than those which have prevailed during the last
few decades. The lack in this direction has been of
organization. The moral forces in distribution have
not been distinctively social forces, but have acted
sporadically upon individuals.

For the present we have to consider the brute
forces of distribution. The employer is, as we have
seen, the purchaser of the laborer's share of a sub-
product. In the transaction capital is necessarily a
unit. Whether the employer be an individual or a
corporation, it is as though there were but one man
wielding the force of the entire capital of a productive establishment, in the effort to secure advanta-
geous terms from the workmen. If, now, the workmen
act not collectively, but individually, if they compete
vigorously with each other for employment, they divide their forces against themselves, assist the capitalist, and forfeit all hope of a successful issue of the
contest. The army of labor fires, as it were, into its
own ranks. The distributive phenomena of the past
have been distinctively those of unbalanced competition.

The strategic inequality in the position of capitalists and laborers would be at a maximum if there were
but one employer in a locality, and if employés were
numerous, unorganized, and unable to migrate. If,
in addition to this, the ethico-economic rule of "every
man for himself" were a recognized principle of action, the result would be a society composed, indeed,

of men, but completely dehumanized in its organic
action. It would be a collective brute.

Such a condition was not fully realized, but was
approximated during the period of declining wages.
The degree of approximation sufficed to reduce wages
to a starvation limit. There was some competition
among employers; their shops were small and relatively numerous. There was an appreciable chance
of realizing the condition described by Cobden, by
the formula, "two bosses after one man"; but this
chance was indefinitely more than offset by the greater
frequency and intensity of the struggles of the men
to secure employment from the "one boss."

Aside from the greater unity of action on the side
of capital, there was a source of unfairness in the distributive contest in the unequal motives of the competitors on the different sides. The impulse to raise
wages never equalled the impulse to depress them.
The employers had less at stake in the struggle to
enlarge their working forces, than had the laborers
in the contest for employment. The man without
work must obtain it or starve; the employer with
too few hands must content himself with smaller
gains than he would like to realize. The man having to choose between something and nothing, might
soon be compelled to take half-pay. On the other
hand, employers, even in the prosperous seasons in
which they compete with each other for men, have

no interest in raising wages to the extent of lessening their aggregate profits; and this point is usually
reached after a relatively moderate rise.   Employment at half-pay might save a man from starvation;
but the payment of double wages would, in most
cases, speedily bankrupt the employer.

If these sources of inequality, even in the age of
small industries, left to the laborers nothing but a
precarious subsistence, what was to be expected from
centralization?   In each producing centre, a score of
little shops have yielded to a single great establishment, and if the laborers had remained unorganized,
the competitive process would have been thrown
more hopelessly out of balance; strife among employers to secure workmen would have been lessened,
and that among men to secure employment would
have been increased.   In addition to this the spirit
of the market has undergone a change; conservative
influences have been thrown off, and the struggle
for gain has become undisguised and intense.   Under
such circumstances, the fate of the workingman, were
he acting in isolation, would indeed be sealed; his
condition would be determined by a struggle of
brute forces, and these would stand as ten to one
against him.   Yet the historical fact of the past
half-century has been that the workman's condition
has improved.   He has thriven on centralization and
an intense struggle for existence.

Of the two possible causes of higher wages both
have been in action in recent years; there has been
more to divide, and the division has been made under
more equal conditions.   The influence with which
we are immediately concerned is the equalization
which has taken place in the brute forces of distribution.   A more nearly balanced competition has
replaced the former one-sided process.   Massed labor
has been pitted against massed capital, by trades
unions, and by the more recent and general union of
the Knights of Labor, which aims — with what permanent result remains to be seen — to secure the
solidarity of the entire working class.

It will be seen that the twofold process of first
throwing competition out of balance and then restoring its equilibrium, has had the effect of ruling a great
part of it out of existence.   The equality has been
secured, not by restoring competition on the side of
capital, but by suppressing it on the side of labor.
As the growth of a great corporation, absorbing all
small establishments in a locality, suppresses competition among employers, the growth of a well-organ-
ized trades union suppresses it among workmen.   If
both processes were consummated, and one corporation
produced the entire supply of a particular article, while
a trades union controlled the entire labor force available for its production, actual competition would be at
an end, and the division of the product would be effected

by a bargaining process untempered by any of the conservative influences by which, in an open market,
contracts are actually made.   There would be no alternative buyers and sellers ; the laborers would be compelled to sell their share of the product to the one
corporate employer; and that employer would be
compelled to buy the product of the trades union,
which, in a sense, is a single corporate laborer.   The
adjustment, if left to be effected by crude force, would
produce disturbances too disastrous to be tolerated, and
arbitration on a comprehensive scale would be a prime
necessity.

This condition is, as yet, only approximated.   The
solidarity of labor and capital is very incomplete.   Corporations have not become absolute monopolies in their
respective fields ; trades unions do not include all workmen.   The bargaining process between capital and labor
is not the blind and desperate struggle that it might be.
It is tending towards that condition, and becoming, in
a corresponding degree, dependent on arbitration.

The solidarity of labor has developed, first, in the line
of occupation, and, secondly, in a line independent of
occupation.   Trades unions are old; the organization
of the Knights of Labor is new.   They represent
respectively two distinct economic conditions, of which
the one is characteristic of the past and the other of
the present.   In the one condition trades are dominant
in the field of industry ; in the other they are of reduced
importance.

The factory system, with its differentiation of manufacturing processes, has given to the term skilled labor a significance quite distinct from that which formerly attached to it. The difference between the skilled and the unskilled workman was once largely personal. The one had attained, by a long course of industrial education, a mental and physical status which made him, for economic purposes, a different being from the other. Native endowment played a large part in broadening the line of demarcation ; men adopted trades for which nature, hereditary or otherwise, had fitted them, and attained a success beyond the reach of the personally unfit. The subdivision of labor has reduced the differences between trades, by reducing the trades themselves to a minimum. The occupation of watch-maker once involved an ability to make an entire watch ; and the person who could perform this difficult industrial function was in no danger of competition from any but the few who, like himself, had been able to serve the needed apprenticeship. This trade, in the full sense, no longer exists. In its place are a score of far simpler trades, each limited to the performance of a minute portion of the watch-making process. The functions requiring especial deftness and accuracy have been handed over to machines, and the difficulty of becoming a member of the watch-producing group has been reduced to a minimum. Though the occupation now demands far less of personal superiority, native and acquired, than was formerly necessary, yet, on the other hand, it develops greater actual dexterity. The little that the artisan now does he does exceedingly well. In a sense, therefore, nearly all the labor engaged in manufacturing processes is highly skilled; yet but little of it requires the personal attainments which were necessary under the old regime.

The subdivision of trades is not equally practicable in all departments, and some occupations still demand skilled labor in the original sense of the term. It is noticeable that in such occupations trades unions are especially vigorous. No industrial development has yet lessened the skill and the moral quality required of a good locomotive engineer, and the brotherhood of men of this craft is one of the strongest of the guilds. Building trades, type-setting, and not a few other employments, are conducted by methods so similar to those which prevailed in the old era as to furnish a basis for vigorous organizations within the lines drawn by occupation.

Where, however, the subdivision of trades has proceeded to considerable lengths, the effect has been to lessen the efficiency of the trades union for the purpose for which it was designed. It can less easily control the market for a particular kind of labor. The brotherhood of locomotive engineers has a certain control of the market for its own kind of labor, because its membership includes a large majority of those who practise the craft, and because the difficulty of acquiring the art renders new men for a long time useless.

In trades which have been so subdivided that the mastership of a few simple operations is all that is required of one workman, the case is different. The members of a craft like this stand more nearly on a plane with the army of the unskilled. Though a union were to embrace all who now practise such an occupation, it would be impossible to include all who are capable of practising it after a brief apprenticeship. It certainly cannot include all the Chinese, Hungarians, and Italians. In most cases it by no means includes all Americans who are now masters of the trade; and a strike, though sustained by the entire brotherhood, cannot compel an employer to make concessions, unless it can prevent him from resorting to the reserve force of the unemployed. For the preventing of such a resort there are two methods: first, coercion, crude or refined, which shall prevent men from taking the places vacated by striking craftsmen; and secondly, the formation of a labor organization which shall proceed independently of occupation, and endeavor ultimately to include the reserve force from which, during a strike, the employer may draw a new quota of men.

Both of the above methods are now in operation; potent influences deter non-union men from accepting work while a strike is pending; and a strong effort is making to unite all labor in a general guild.   The novel feature of the former process is the use of the boycott. This is a mode of coercion applied to employers, not only for the purpose of extorting direct concessions from them, but for the purpose of indirectly coercing the non-union men.   The object for which it is most frequently used is to compel employers to retain only members of the guild in their service.   The coercive agency consists in the cutting off of the market for the employer's products.

Were these products sold directly to the workmen, a sufficiently extensive labor union could effectually boycott the producer by simply refraining from the purchase of the articles.   In most cases the direct customers for the goods do not belong to the working class, and the boycott, in order to reach the producer, must attack the retailers who sell his products.   These are numerous, and a boycott which passes only to the second degree must often coerce scores of men in order to extort the desired concession from one.   Yet boycotts of the third degree are frequent.   A newspaper is coerced by compelling the withdrawal of profitable advertisements; if the advertisers are manufacturers, they must be reached through the retail dealers.

The ultimate weakness of the boycott, as an instrument for benefiting the laborer, lies in the necessity for thus widening the circle within which it is applied. The disturbances created by it are out of all proportion

to the ends secured.   In slightly benefiting a class, it
inflicts a large injury upon society.   Even more than
the strike does the boycott need to be held in reserve,
with masterly strategy, and seldom actually applied.
The ultimate power to boycott, if skilfully used by the
director of a labor organization, may force many concessions from employers; the frequent application of
the force must speedily defeat its own ends.   The surprising degree of success which the boycotting system
in its early stages attained, is not to be anticipated
hereafter, unless it is used with consummate wisdom.
It is ruinous policy to push it beyond what may be
termed the tolerance of society.

The success of the boycott, when kept within pru-
dent limits, lies wholly in the power of federated labor
to dictate the conduct of retail dealers; and this power
is based on competition.   It is the existence of rival
dealers that is the decisive fact in the situation.   The
boycott promises to benefit the dealer who submits to
it, at the cost of all who resist.   The labor union ap-
proaches the retailer not merely with a threat, but also
with a promise.   If A complies with its demand while
B, C, D, and E resist, the union will turn to A's shop
a large part of the patronage of the other four.   An
anti-boycott union among retail dealers needs to be
universal, in order to be effective; and, in the absence
of such a complete concert of action, a merchant of
this class is interested to secure, by a prompt surrender

to the boycotters, an immunity from harm and a possible benefit. If fully organized, retailers might be
capable of valor in an encounter with labor unions;
as unorganized, they, as a rule, strive only to outdo
each other in discretion.

Even when the ends for which it is used are economic, the boycott, as an instrument, is extra-economic
and definitely illegal. Narrow policy on the part of
laborers demands an exceedingly limited use of it;
broad policy dictates a line of conduct identical with
that demanded by morality, and that is the total suppression of the practice. From this time onward the
success of labor unions depends on the strength of their
moral position; and it is indefinitely better for them
to voluntarily relinquish an illegal practice than to be
forced to do so by officers of the law.

Rapidly as organizations of workmen have lately
grown, the solidarity of capital is, thus far, greater than
that of labor. Eight men have been said to control the
production of anthracite coal, and combinations of
similar character control that of lumber, glass, nails,
gunpowder, rope, cutlery, and a hundred other staple
articles. In the language of our formulas, the non-competing groups are solidifying into great corporations;
and as competition between the producers of dissimilar
sub-products is impossible by nature, that between the
makers and vendors of the same sub-product is being
suppressed by art. Nail-makers cannot compete with

cloth-makers, and they do not compete with each other.

The object of these combinations is to control the prices of products. They operate in what we have termed the primary and secondary fields of distribution, while labor unions operate in the ternary. Employers combine against the public, and workmen against employers. The associations of capitalists are able to act directly against striking and boycotting workmen, and are, indeed, beginning to do so. This is, however, a new field for their action; and even in their original field their operation reacts in two ways upon real wages.

The raising of the price of a commodity produced by a confederation of employers is possible only by curtailing production. If the price is raised while production is unrestrained, goods accumulate till forced sales are necessary, and the combination is broken.

It is for the interest of every group that its production of commodities should be small, and that of other groups large. In that case the terms of exchange between the one group and the others will be favorable to this particular group. By making less nails one particular class of producers secure for themselves more food, clothing, etc. Of course this is at the cost of the other groups, and when they retaliate by a curtailment of their own production, the gain of the nail-makers is more than neutralized, and new injuries are inflicted on all. Under free competition the production of each commodity tends towards a normal quantitative limit, at which point labor is, with allowance for certain variations, as well rewarded in that industry as in others. If a single industrial group were to curtail its production beyond the normal limit, it might gain, but society would suffer; while the outcome of a general artificial curtailment would be a general social injury.

The gain which comes to a particular group by a lessening of its production accrues mainly to employers; the injury which it suffers from a similar action on the part of other groups falls largely on the men. If nail-producers can so limit their output as to secure a price higher by a half than the one formerly prevailing, they can retain most of the gain for themselves. Wages in this single industry cannot be greatly raised independently of the general labor market. A demand made at the moment when the price of nails rises may give to the workmen a portion of the gain realized by their producing group; but the gain cannot raise these workmen far above the level of others, while the increase of the employer's profits may be much greater.

On the other hand, the workmen suffer most from the injury which is entailed upon society by artificial restrictions upon production. They are preëminently consumers. They compose a large numerical proportion of society; they consume the largest portion

of their incomes, and they spend it largely for things
which they cannot forego without privation. For these
three reasons they are specially sensitive to the injury
resulting from enhanced prices of articles of ordinary
consumption.

There is a second way in which employers' combinations react detrimentally upon wages. A curtailment
of the production of a particular commodity means a
lessened demand for labor within the group which
produces it. A struggle between the groups to outdo
each other in limiting production would mean, to the
laborers, an effort on the part of each group to thrust
laboring men into other groups. As the attempt
becomes general, the result is a thrusting of laborers
either into the reserve force of the unemployed, or into
the one department in which employers' combinations
are impossible, namely, agriculture. The power of
agricultural industry to absorb the working force excluded from other fields is becoming limited, and the
army of the unemployed must receive an increasing
proportion of them. The reaction of this fact upon the
reward of labor is direct and resistless; no combination
of workmen can undo the depressing effect upon their
own wages of the presence of a large force of idle men.
Upon the men thrown out of employment the effect of
curtailed production is obvious; it is equally so upon
society. It means pauperism, crime, embittered contests, and an added strain upon republicanism.

Although it was not the original object of employers' unions to directly oppose trades unions, the present tendency of labor movements is to make it morally certain that they will be used for that purpose. This wholesale suppression of competition will bring society to a point from which the only outcome consistent with peace will be arbitration under governmental authority. Rapid progress in this direction is the great economic fact of the present day. Competition still exists and, within certain fields, is active. There is competitive action among merchants, among railroads not in a pool, among manufacturers not in a combination, and among workmen outside of a union. Moreover, the latent possibility of competition among the members of a combination is an economic fact of vast importance to society. Yet the fact remains that, in the field where its work is the most important, in the division of the products of industry between groups, sub-groups and classes, competition of the individualistic type is rapidly passing out of existence. The principle which is at the basis of Ricardian economics is ceasing to have any general application to the system under which we live.

The problem of the future is the extent to which movements now in progress will actually go. In their possible scope they are highly revolutionary. Solidarity carried to its logical consummation would create a social condition so utterly unlike the present one that

it could hardly be established without violent overturn-
ings.

The immediate subject for economic study is the condition to which the movement has already brought us.
The present state of industrial society is transitional
and chaotic. The consolidation of labor is incomplete,
that of capital is so; and the relation between the two
is not what it was yesterday, nor what it will be
to-morrow. Yet something may be said of social conditions existing in the interim between the old and the
new. The crudeness of the transitional system has
begotten lawlessness. Labor is employing irregular
methods in the contest with capital; capital is using
injurious methods in its dealings with society. Individual competition, the great regulator of the former
era, has, in important fields, practically disappeared.
It ought to disappear; it was, in its latter days, incapable of working justice. The alternative regulator
is moral force, and this is already in action. It is
accomplishing much, though it is in the infancy of its
distinctively social development. The system of individualistic competition was a tolerated and regulated
reign of force; solidarity, even in its present crude
state, presents the beginnings of a reign of law.

CHAPTER IX.

THE ETHICS OF TRADE.

A WORKING MAN, who is well versed in political economy, once told me that the reading of Ricardo had convinced him that there is no hope for the laboring class under the existing system of industry. Competition, as he was compelled to think, must sooner or later reduce workmen to the starvation limit, and keep them there. In times of exceptional distress, it must drive them below that limit, and only restore them to it through the lessening of their number by actual death. His hopes for the future of his class were founded on a change in the industrial system, which should substitute coöperation for competition.

This man is representative; his premises are those of Ricardo and his school, and his conclusions are those to which many readers are forced.* This fact explains the popularity of orthodox economic literature among declared socialists. It prepares the soil for revolutionary seed. A demonstration of the hopelessness of the old economic system is, to a man who retains his natural optimism, equivalent to a proof that a new system is coming. The new era has, in fact, begun, but it has not brought socialism.

---

* Ricardo's own conclusion was different; his "natural price of labor" was not literally a starvation rate.

The weakness of Ricardianism is known to lie in its premises; these are sweeping assumptions at variance with the facts of life. It may now be seen that the fundamental principle of this scientific system, that of free individual competition, is not permanent, and that the industrial regime to which the old science was intended to apply is self-terminating. There is a promise of an industrial revolution in the very laws of Ricardianism.

The purely competitive system of industry has had its youth, its manhood and its decrepitude. It has developed, first, a conservative rivalry, then a sharp and destructive contest, and, finally, a movement toward consolidation and monopoly. The final stage has but lately been reached, and the system of distribution which characterizes it is, as yet, imperfectly developed.

Moral force as an economic agent is the characteristic of the new regime. This agent is new only in the field of its operation and in the extent of its work. In itself it is an old and ultra-orthodox economic force. It is a radical error which represents competition itself as the outworking of unmixed selfishness. There is an element of morality in it; it is a restrained and qualified strife, and owes such continuance as it has had to the forces that have held it within bounds. An unrestricted struggle for wealth is impossible in any collection of men that can be termed a society; it has never existed, in fact, since the time of Adam. It would be a savage

and ignoble strife, in which every man's hand would be
against his neighbor. Deprive a pack of wolves of the
tribal instinct that keeps them from rending each other,
and place a single carcass before them, and their conduct may illustrate the economic system which would
result from the unrestrained action of selfish motives
among men.

Competition without moral restraints is a monster as
completely antiquated as the saurians of which the geol-
ogists tell us. To find anything approaching it in actual
life we must go farther back than history reaches, beyond the lake-dwellers of Switzerland and the cliff
villagers of neolithic times, quite to the isolated troglodyte, the companion of the cave bear. Even here the
illustration will be incomplete; for the troglodyte had a
family, and, within the precinct of his home, was ruled by
higher motives. The intercourse of this rudest of men
with others of his kind may, however, be conceded,
safely enough, in the absence of evidence to the contrary, to have been dictated by the lowest of motives,
and to have tolerably well illustrated the process of
unrestrained competition. The supposition may be a
slander on the troglodyte; but as he is now past hearing of it, and is not present with his club to avenge it,
we may admit the supposition that the intercourse of
the isolated cave-dwellers with each other presented an
illustration of competitive strife unqualified by moral
forces. Two wild huntsmen pursuing the same animal,

and then clubbing and tearing each other for the possession of its body, may illustrate the process.

Though such may have been the conduct of cave-
dwellers toward each other outside of the family circle,
it is certain that, within that circle, the passions elsewhere predominant were restrained by sentiments of
affection; and in this we have the germ of a series of
most important phenomena. In this case love toward
relatives and enmity toward neighbors are the ruling
motives. The differing motives dictate opposite lines
of conduct. Reflection serves to define and formulate
the two opposite modes of action; that which is cus-
tomary in the treatment of relatives and that which is
characteristic in the treatment of enemies come to be
understood and recognized, and a rude code of rules is
formed for the guidance of numbers of the favored
circle in their treatment of each other. Gradually,
from the depths of a nascent faculty of reason, a deeper
intuition than any yet experienced comes to lay its
sanction on the code which family affection and custom
have established. In the vivid picture-language of
Genesis, the fruit of " the tree of knowledge of good and
evil " is plucked. A rude perception of right and wrong
is attained. The glimmering light of a moral principle
that is to direct the development of the race makes
itself for the first time perceptible, and the troglodyte
is no longer as an animal, innocent because ignorant,
but "as a god, knowing good and evil." Such is,

perhaps, the teaching of Genesis and the guess of science concerning the origin of moral influences in human society.

The code of right and wrong is, at first, confined to the family; but in time sufficiently close intercourse is established between neighboring families to develop common ideas of right and wrong in matters pertaining to a larger circle, and the moral code extends itself to the neighborhood. Neighborhoods unite into tribes, and the process repeats itself. In time the final step is taken; the moral code receives the sanction of a legal enactment, with penalties for violation, and is thus enabled to exert its greatest influence. The competitive system has now received definite limitations within the circle where the ethical influences are exerted.

The growth of these influences, in both an extensive and an intensive way, is a matter of history. They have grown extensively as tribes have united into nations, and as nations, by the development of international law, have taken on the rudimentary form of what promises to be a world state, an organic unity bounded by no narrower limits than those of the globe we inhabit. There is no quarter of the world, at present, unreached by ethical influences, and none, consequently, where the competitive impulse is not subject to some limitations.

Intensively these moral forces have grown with general

civilization, acquiring, within a given local circle, a constantly increasing power, and restricting the wealth-getting process more and more. The crude competition which spared neither life nor limb gave place to a method which respected the lives of the contestants; murder, as an economic process, was prohibited, while robbery was still tolerated. Human bodies were first excluded from the list of articles to be competed for. It was a sort of legal exemption, the first and most beneficent of homestead laws. The dwelling which the soul of man inhabits might not be seized by his creditors and the occupant ejected.

A farther moral development extended the protection of the law to outward possessions, suppressing first open robbery, and then obvious fraud, and extending its influence ultimately to those refined forms of coercion and deceit of which a large survival remains to be dealt with.

From the time when the institution of property was put upon a moral basis the nature of the competitive process changed. In the primitive state it was a struggle to secure a *de facto* possession; in the civilized state it is a struggle to secure lawful possession. This is possible only by creating something of value, or by receiving it from a previous owner by a voluntary cession. Useful articles are not relinquished without an inducement; and here is the basis of the system of exchanges which is the distinctive phenomenon of civilized society.

Those who desire an article of value must seek to outdo each other in offering to its possessor inducements to part with it. Rivalry in giving is, therefore, the essence of legitimate competition. It is the function of moral influences to see to it that the process retains this character; it is, in fact, constantly losing it, and lapsing into the cruder state. The refinements of force and fraud which are beyond the reach of statute law, are still used in securing *de facto* possession without moral right. Competition, in the new era, is indeed debarred from certain extensive fields; but in others it survives, and it is of vital importance that its methods be made legitimate.

Sir Henry Maine has shown that the family system, which excluded competition entirely, extended itself to the village community, which was the germ of the modern state. Within the village all relations were fraternal, and property was held largely in common; while on the mark, or boundary, the germ of the modern market, the relations were somewhat hostile. It was on the mark that members of different communities met to buy and sell. Here they were free from the moral influences which existed among members of the same community, and mercantile processes were, therefore, relatively unrestrained. Here there was "higgling," the contention between buyers and sellers; though there was but little of that true competition, the rivalry in giving, which is the character-istic of modern trade.

The highly developed family code acquired its greatest field of action in the mediæval village. The local circle within which mercantile action is excluded has been reduced to a zero; but, in com-pensation, much of the humanity which characterized the dealings of villagers with each other has extended itself to all members of society in their non-mercantile relations. The mark, as such, is now extinct; and, in western countries, the village community is so. Modern society consists of a fusion of the two, and bears the stamp of each of the elements that com-pose it. In some of its activities the modern com-munity resembles the mark; in others it resembles the village. This dualism is most apparent and most harmful in the domain of practical morals.

The tribal conscience formerly developed fine sensi-bilities; the inter-tribal conscience was cruder, and tolerated mercantile contention and the recognized " tricks of trade." The man of the present day is actuated, now by one influence, and now by the other, and has two distinct codes of outward conduct. Moral philosophy, indeed, teaches that his fundamental character is one and unchanging; but as there is one code of practical conduct for peace and another for war, so there is one code for the family, the social circle, and the church, and a different one for mercantile life. The man of business is constantly passing from the jurisdiction of the one code to that of the other. Even the laws of war are improving, with the general growth of moral influences; and the quasi-martial laws of trade are subject to similar improvement. Progress in this respect is not uniform; there are periods when it is checked by the action of sharp competition. From such a period we are now emerging, and a reformation of the morals of trade affords the chief hope of a better industrial condition.

It is a common remark, that business practices are not what they should be, and that a sensitive conscience must be left at home when its possessor goes to the office or the shop. We helplessly deprecate this fact; we lament the forms of business depravity that come to our notice, but attack them with little confidence. We are appalled by the great fact of the moral dualism in which we live, and are inclined to resign ourselves to the necessity of a twofold life. We do not realize that moral influences have for their particular and legitimate function to suppress the remnants of natural ferocity which show themselves in the economic dealings of man with man; neither do we realize how radical would be the effect of a comparatively slight reformation in this direction. Religion has held itself too much aloof from this particular work; and so effectual has been, at times, the separation of religious life from business life that seeming piety has, in too many cases, been consistent with business meanness. Such is the bitter moral fruit of the competitive system.

It was the effort of mediæval times to secure, by public sentiment and by positive statutes, a reign of just prices in all commercial dealings. This precluded, to a great extent, the effort of rival sellers of commodities to secure custom for themselves by offering their products for less than the established rates. Similar causes repressed competition in the labor market. Yet it is not true that the competitive principle was not then in action. In legislating to enforce just prices, the law-makers had a criterion for determining what was just. Custom, in the main, furnished this criterion, and this was itself determined by a certain latent and unconscious process of competition. If the rule of just prices were to be introduced at present, and open rivalry in buying and selling suppressed, there would still be need of the criterion of justice, and the latent competition would again have its work to do. The ethico-economic fact of the mediæval period, and, let us hope, of the coming period, is the recognition of the duty of all to conform to the standard of justice thus established.

From the mediæval stage competition has developed through two distinct conditions. The former of these is that in which law of just prices still rules in transactions outside of the general market, but in which the attempt to control the market itself by moral or statutory regulations is abandoned. Within the theatre of general exchanges the standard is set by the undisguised efforts of many persons to outdo each other in offering products to society as the general consumer. Turn the market into a general auction; let sellers do their best in underbidding each other in price, which is overbidding in service rendered; note the results in the prices current, and then abide by them in separate individual dealings; such is the mercantile code in the second stage of development.

This code is imperfectly obeyed; and, as violations of it become frequent, they react on the ethical rule itself. The third stage of competitive development is characterized by the gradual abandonment of the rule which requires that the individual should, in isolated transactions, conform to market standards. The new practice allows a man to get what he can by trade, under any and all circumstances. The system becomes as undisguisedly predatory as one can be without violating the rights of property in actual possession. The man who buys for less than the market price or sells for more is held to have done a creditable action.

The theory of the modern bargain appears to be that of the mediæval judicial combat: let each do his worst, and God will protect the right. As in

mediæval times providence has often protected the
wrong, and, by this means, revealed the abominations
of the system. There is a standard which determines
the justice or injustice of bargains; and though the
" higgling of the market" in which competition is
general secures a rude conformity to that standard,
that which takes place between a buyer and a seller
isolated from competitors stands in no relation to
it. Here is a chief seat of business depravity. The
Scriptures are full of references to unjust bargaining;
ancient law-givers attacked it; the codes of the middle ages endeavored to suppress it, but moralists of
recent years have sighed and resigned themselves to
wait a geological era for moral influences to become
strong enough to uproot the evil. It has been
entrenched in the competitive system; with recent
changes in that system it has become open to
attack. If there is an intelligible law determining
the moral quality of business dealings, it is time that
it were universally taught and a just standard
enforced.

Wealth is legitimately acquired by the operation of
production, not by that of exchange. We have already
endeavored to draw the line where production termi-
nates. An exchange made at rates current in an open
market makes neither party richer; it is mutually ad-
vantageous and morally commendable. A bargain
which enriches one party at the expense of the other

must deviate, in its terms, from current standards. Money-making by exchange is virtual robbery, and is only prevented from being legal robbery by the imperfection of the law.

Intelligent persons do not need to be told that dealing in commodities as the merchant deals in them is an operation which falls, scientifically, under the head of production. The merchant creates form utility, place utility, and time utility; and his reward is as legitimate as that of any other producer. He has numerous opportunities for passing beyond his normal function, and acquiring wealth by exchange; but this is always by unfair dealing. If he buys in gross, sells in detail, and gives honest goods for an honest price, he is as much a producer as a farmer or an artisan.

It is the shrewd trading men who create no wealth, but deal in stocks, produce, real estate, horses, etc., in a manner that benefits no one but themselves, that furnish the best illustrations of money-making by the operation of exchange. Market prices are nothing to such men; it is their aim to get more value than they give, both in buying and in selling. As this is not easy when the parties with whom they deal are aware of the value of the property to be transferred, it comes to pass that lying is a frequent part of the process. The mercantile lie is the chief modern instrument for getting wealth without creating it. The falsehood had better not be, in most cases, bald and obvious; it would then be a crude instrument ill adapted to modern uses. It needs to be a refined product, adapted to the system of which it is a part.

What is ordinarily termed a good bargain is, morally, a bad bargain. It is unequal, and good for one party only. Whenever such a transaction takes place, some one is plundered. We should term a purchase or a sale good only when it conforms to the standard of equity; we actually call it so when it departs from that standard, and we gauge its goodness by the amount of the departure. It is the sufferer by such a transaction who usually regrets it; in an ideal society it would be the gainer who would mourn. Sackcloth and ashes are the proper covering of the man who has made a good bargain. What is the fact in the case? Do the men who have gained something by this questionable means don the garments of humiliation? Do they feel shame, or complacency? Are they disposed to conceal their action, or to boast of it? Are they, in fact, treated with less honor by other men, or with more? The whole process is bad; it is odious, and the worst feature of it is that it is characteristically American.

The sharp bargaining spirit which seeks to get wealth away from its possessors by all methods tolerated by law, is characteristic of the degenerate days of the competitive system. Moral influence is more powerful and pervasive in America than in most countries; and if public sentiment among us renders sharp trading respectable, it is due to the fact that competition has degenerated earlier here than elsewhere.

The man who, in Germany, France, or England, should go from shop to shop to find whose prices were the lowest would be, if not turned out of doors, at least treated in such a manner that he would go, and not return. A certain survival of the mediæval code, the tradition of a time when the just price was the legal rule, has prevented the men of these countries from living up to the logic of the competitive system in its final stage. In America we are more consistent; we accept the results of a degenerate competition, greatly to the detriment of our morality. Trade is actually held in greater honor here than elsewhere, and it deserves to be held in less; a part of our respect for it is due to our peculiar blindness to its defects. Let us withhold our respect until it is due, and, that we may justly honor trade, let us make it honorable.

A perfect ideal of character and conduct usually serves the purpose rather of a beacon than of a goal. Like the star toward which the sailor steers, it is a thing never to be reached, but only distantly approached. Yet the pilot who depends on a star for direction is in peril of life if he loses sight of it; and something similar to this is true of a society which loses from view its moral ideal. No fog ever baffled

a sailor more completely than the dual code of morality, the outgrowth of a degenerate mercantile system,
has blinded and baffled the people of this country.
The true standard of business dealing has been hid;
it needs to be brought to the light and placed where
all may see it. Though it were never reached, it
would make all the difference between success and
failure, if our course could be turned toward it instead
of from it.

The changes now in progress make it possible to do
more than to gaze at the moral ideal of trade from a
hopeless distance, or even to somewhat lessen the
gulf that separates us from it. Moral force is to
work, hereafter, from a new vantage-ground. There
is, moreover, among the multitude of those whose
occupations are wholly legitimate, and whose con-
sciences are not blinded by the false mercantile code
that has begun to prevail among us, a moral energy
amply adequate to accomplish the reformation of our
business system, could the true principles of practical
ethics be generally taught and accepted.

One form of business immorality is very radical in
its effects, and the removal of it would be more than
a palliative for existing social evils; it would be, to a
great extent, curative. The evil is the most savage
form of competitive action tolerated by law. Much
of our bargaining is a refinement of fraud; this is a
refinement of highway robbery. It is a survival of

troglodyte economy, though its methods are adapted
to the civilized state. The aim of the practice is to
get property by force from weak possessors. The
weapon used is not the club of the cave-dweller; it
is unnecessary to kill the victim; it is only necessary
to present to him an alternative so hard as to compel
him to relinquish his possessions. The matching of
strength against weakness is contrary to fighting codes;
equal armor and equal weapons were the rule of
knighthood. The mercantile code permits any amount
of inequality of outfit. We need a revival of the old
German sense of honor; and especially and particularly do we need a little of that chivalrous spirit
which protected women and children in mediæval
times. It is one of the enigmas of modern life that
the literal striking of a woman, however lightly, should
brand the offender as a social outcast, while, in an
economic way, the deadliest blows may be struck at
her with impunity; and that society even honors men
who get rich by such unknightly attacks on the de-
fenceless. The modern sense of personal honor is,
like the modern standard of morality, dualistic.

Special exigencies often render particular persons
unable to bargain on equal terms with those with
whom they are dealing. They may be compelled to
sell something immediately, and the urgency of the
case may allow no time to seek more than one purchaser. They are, for the time being, excluded from

any general market. In this case, as in most cases, freedom unqualified by law is not freedom, but license. The commercial code which authorizes a trader to depart from the standards furnished by the general market gives him, as it were, letters of marque, authorizing him to prey upon the weak at will.

A borrower, in special exigencies, is often at the mercy of a single lender. A merchant who is in any danger of failing in business is often compelled to accept the offer of a single customer. A land-owner who cannot pay his mortgages is often compelled to accept what a single purchaser may choose to offer; and men are numerous enough whose business it is to create and to utilize such exigencies. The actual creation of the exigencies is most frequently the business of the operator in the stock exchange or the produce exchange; but the utilizing of them is common enough everywhere. It is the baldest of robbery, and is all the worse because the law cannot reach it effectively. The result of recent movements is to lessen the field for it, and, with public sentiment acting in the right direction, we may hope for the correction of the evil.

In other than financial exigencies the true principle is clearly enough recognized. A boatman does not stop to make terms with a man in the water before taking him on board. A ship's captain does not settle the question of salvage before taking the crew

from a wreck. They render the service without question, and collect the equitable reward afterwards.
Society demands the prompt rendering of the service;
the refusal to render it is a crime, and the making of
conditions is a temporary refusal. The boatman who
bargains with a sinking man, virtually says to him, "I
now refuse to rescue you, but will change my mind if
you will give me a certain sum. My refusal to rescue
you is equivalent to drowning you, and I shall drown
you unless you give me some something to which I
have no equitable claim." It is the position of the
highwayman; and the same is true of those who utilize
financial exigencies in the same way. Financial
drowning brings ruin to families, and is sometimes as
much worse, in its effects, than literal drowning, as
the slow starvation of many persons, or their intellectual and moral ruin, is worse than the quick death
of one person. The moral and legal principle is the
same in both cases, and should be equally recognized
and obeyed.

It is too much to expect that persons whose nature
prompts them to a predatory commercial life will change
their practices while the field continues open for them.
The hope for a radical change in this department
of business ethics lies partly in the fact that the
field is no longer clear for the worst practices which
the competitive system has developed. Where a
mercantile freebooter gains an advantage by the

methods above described, his rivals feel compelled to adopt them, against the protest of their moral nature, and competition tends to level the mercantile community downward to the moral standard which proves most profitable. It is a very ordinary honesty which is the best policy, in a time of unscrupulous competition.

The chief bearing of these principles is upon the labor questions of the day. Workmen have heretofore been the most frequent victims of predatory competition. Large numbers of them have been practically confined to one employer, as a customer for that which they have had to sell. Their exigency has often been extreme, and their relations to each other such that, when cases of extreme need have occurred, the effect has been diffused over the entire number. Not only the few whose necessities have compelled them to accept whatever was offered, but the entire class which they represent, have been liable, at such times, to have their wages lowered. It is, as a rule, by means of a few exceptional cases that the extreme results of unbalanced competition are suffered by the laboring class; and it takes place by a process of rotation, in which, at every step, advantage is taken by some one of isolated cases of distress.

A few persons are at first crowded out of employment; a brief period suffices to reduce these to a condition where they must accept anything which may be offered for their labor. If some one who is on the watch for such opportunities now offers them half the prevailing rate, and they accept it, the effect may be to displace others, and to reduce them also, by the hunger argument, to a willingness to accept a similar reduction. The process may be repeated indefinitely, until, in the end, general wages are correspondingly reduced. The many benevolent employers who engage in the procedure with reluctance are driven to it by the competition of others. A few men without employment, and a few employers without souls, are the conditions of a general reduction of wages below the point to which more legitimate causes would reduce them. Unemployed men and soulless employers always exist somewhere. It was stated, in the interest of railroad managers, at the time of the general strike of 1877, that the places of the strikers could all have been filled, at the reduced rate which was then offered; and it was on this supposition that much denunciation was expended on the leaders of the movement. On general principles the statement is very improbable. The vacancies could have been filled, had they occurred a few at a time, by the process of rotation above described; but, after the changes had taken place, it would have been, to a great extent, the same men who would have been found in the positions. A few at a time they would have left their employment, suffered for a while, and returned to their work.

This rapid rotation, whereby large classes are reduced to a rate of wages lower than that at which they can permanently live, lower than any to which legitimate causes would need to reduce them, is the only means whereby, in a country like ours, the extreme results of Ricardo's principle can be realized. It has never, in our actual experience, been realized. We have seen wave after wave of competition, sharper than that which exists in other countries, sweep over the industrial classes, beginning with retail dealers, and extending itself to wholesale dealers and manufacturers, until it has reached the laboring class, and spent its accumulated strength upon them. Yet wages have rebounded, after each depression, to a level above that which is maintained in conservative countries. The cause is obvious, — our vacant lands. Competition cannot starve men while free farms are waiting for them. Yet thoughtful men must have realized that the reward of labor in this country has not been as much above that which has elsewhere prevailed as our resources would have warranted. Something must, in a measure, have neutralized our advantages; and, while causes like an excessive tariff will occur to every one, a part of the effect must be attributed to the sharply competitive spirit of our people. Labor unions have been late in developing, and unbalanced competition, under a low code of commercial ethics, has produced its natural effects.

Free homesteads of good quality are no longer to be had; and this fact radically changes the industrial situation. It lessens the product to be divided between employers and workmen, and it modifies the terms of the division. We must depend on new influences, in both directions, in the era which is coming. If the product of industry is materially lessened, no readjustment of the terms of division between labor and capital can make good the workman's loss. The influence tending to make industry productive we shall later examine; that which favorably affects the terms of distribution is not merely the consolidation of labor, but that movement followed by the moral development for which it opens the way. The solidarity of labor calls imperatively for arbitration, in the adjustment of its claims, and accustoms the public mind to accept a standard of wages determined by justice rather than force. Within broad limits it puts a definite stop to the predatory methods which competition has developed. Soulless employers can no longer use a few unemployed men as a lever with which to reduce the wages of an entire class. The process of rotation, by which this has been possible, is precluded by the establishment of strong trades-unions. The pecuniary effect of this change is of im-

portance to laborers; the moral reaction which it
occasions is of incalculable value to employers. Their
better impulses may now assert themselves. The
employer who has long been willing to pay fair
wages, but has been unable to do so because of his
neighbor's competition, is relieved from his dilemma.
The necessity which compelled him to stifle his conscience is changed to a coercion forcing him to obey
it; and while right conduct under compulsion may
not redeem him in the eyes of the moralist, it removes
a blight from his business life, and makes a truly moral
development possible. To society as a whole the
changes incident to the altered relations of employers
and workmen involve a change of organic character.

The present interval is morally transitional. The
relaxing of healthy restraints, the growth of mercantile license, has characterized the period now closing.
Trade has become openly predatory, and the weak
have been the victims. The field for such practices
has been partly closed, but the code which jus-
tified them has not been abandoned. We are in danger of importing into the new era the ethics of the
old. It would be the anomaly of old wine in new
bottles, the spirit of a decayed system surviving after
its forms had been renewed. With the growth of new
processes of distribution, with arbitration and the
various forms of industrial partnership, a better ethical
code must assert itself. Justice in the division of

products, equality in exchanges, must become the aim
of social effort. The gain will be both material and
moral; the change which makes workmen richer will
make all classes better; and what is of more importance, it will open the way for continued progress.
Wages may sometimes be low, but not because of
an eternal downward tendency; and the death-line
as a natural limit will forever disappear. The
law which condemned society, as an organic whole,
to a career of brutality will be changed to a law
which will open before it a continuous growth in
righteousness.

NOTE. — The foregoing theory of business ethics does not condemn
speculation as such. To buy articles when they are cheap with a
view to selling them when they are dearer, is to acquire wealth by
accretions of time utility, as indicated in Chapter II. The theory
condemns the manipulating of temporary prices by virtual force or
fraud; but the form of immorality to which it refers as characteristic
of a degenerate system is that which appears in the dealings of one
individual with another, and which consists in using refinements of
force or fraud in such a manner as to effect unequal exchanges. The
standard of equity in the purchase and sale of commodities is determined by the normal action of demand and supply in an open market.

CHAPTER X.

THE PRINCIPLE OF COÖPERATION.

HISTORY has lately been said to move in cycles and epicycles; its phenomena tend to recur at intervals, in regular succession. An anarchic condition may be followed by despotism, that by democracy, and that again by anarchy; yet the second anarchy is not like the first; and when it, in turn, yields to despotism, that also is different from the former despotism. The course of history has been in a circle, but it is a circle whose centre is moving. The same phenomena may recur indefinitely; but at each recurrence the whole course of events will have advanced, and the existing condition will have its parallel, though not its precise duplicate, in some previous condition. There is nothing permanent in history, and there is nothing new. That which is will pass away, and that which will take its place will be like something that has already existed and passed away. History moves, like the earth, in an orbit; but, like the earth, it moves in an orbit the centre of which is describing a greater orbit.

That any particular condition has existed in the past, and has passed away, is no evidence that it will not return, but is rather an evidence that it will return, though in a different form. That village-communities working on a coöperative plan existed in the Middle Ages, and that something resembling them existed in antiquity, is, as far as it goes, an evidence that industrial coöperation will return, though in a form adapted to its new surroundings. That a fraternal spirit prevailed where this plan was in operation, and that justice rather than force presided over the distribution of wealth, affords some evidence that this moral force will do a similar work in the modern world. Productive property owned in undivided shares by laboring men, contention over the division of products replaced by general fraternity, — this is the ideal which humanity has repeatedly approached, abandoned, and approached again.

The earlier cycles of the historic movement are too remote for tracing; the records of the last one are reasonably distinct. We have been made familiar, of late, with the village-community of mediæval times. Beginning at that point, we may trace the economic history of Europe through a series of conditions bearing less and less resemblance to the communal ideal, until we reach the aphelion of the system, the point of extreme individualism, and begin slowly to tend in an opposite direction. This turning-point may be located at a period about a hundred years ago. While Adam Smith was formulating the present system of political economy, the world was, in industrial relations, at the extreme limit of individualistic development. The manufacturers of the period were a myriad of capitalist-artisans, each working in his little shop. The common carriers were an army of wagoners. The hired workmen were without union; and every-man-for-himself was the rule among them, as among their employers.

The feature of the next period, which still continues, is a practical movement tending, not to abolish or to weaken the institution of private property, but to vest the ownership of capital in organizations rather than in individuals. These organizations may be private corporations, village-communities, cities, or even states; and if laboring men are represented in them, there is seen, in practical working, a form of coöperation.

The word thus signifies a more highly developed social organization.. Within the great organism which we term the state there are many specific organisms of an industrial character. Such are nearly all our manufactories. These have the marks of high development in a minute differentiation of parts; labor is minutely subdivided in these establishments. One man grinds in the axe-factory, and, during his brief lifetime, is not, in economic relations, an independent being, but only a part of the grinding organ of an axe-making creature whose separate atoms are men. All the laborers of the factory, taken collectively, compose an organism which acts as a unit in the making of axes. This working body, however, with its human molecules, is acting in a subordinate capacity; — it is hired. As a whole it is serving an employer, and it desires to become independent. The same ambition which prompts the apprentice to leave his master, and start in business for himself, is now prompting these organizations of employés to desire a similar promotion. Industrial organisms are seeking what individuals have long been encouraged to seek, — emancipation. It is the old struggle for personal independence, translated to a higher plane of organic life.

The modes in which this end is sought are various; and, in so far as the object is realized by any of them, competition is held in abeyance within the organizations, and the division of the product is determined by justice rather than force.

Justice is by no means excluded under the present system. What we term competition is, in practice, subject to such moral limitations that it can be so termed only in a qualified sense. Moral force, however, within the competitive system, acts only as a restraining influence; it fixes certain limits within which the self-seeking impulses are encouraged to operate, and determine by a struggle the division of the fruits of industry.

The adjustment of wages by arbitration is a departure from this principle, and, wherever adopted, remands competition to a subordinate place. The general prevalence of it would mean a reign of law rather than of force, and would mark an era in the moral evolution of society. The era would, however, be one of quasi-litigation. To be successful, the plan of arbitration requires many tribunals in ceaseless activity. It checks lockouts and strikes, and allays the antagonism excited by these overt conflicts. The speedy establishment of the tribunals is, therefore, the present desideratum. Yet the arbitrative system is not an ideal one. Its fundamental defect lies in the fact that it concentrates the attention of employers and of workmen on the terms of the division of their joint product. An issue of this kind, even though amicably adjusted, tends, in itself, in the direction of antagonism. It fails, moreover, to secure the largest product for division.

Coöperation works in an opposite way in both respects. It concentrates the thought and energy of all on production, the process in which the interests of different classes are identical; and it develops harmony of feeling, while securing a large product for distribution. It avoids the constant readjustment of the terms of division, which is the characteristic of the arbitrative system, and takes the workman permanently out of the position in which his gain is his employer's loss. It makes fraternity possible among men.

Wage workers are now striving, by the crude means at present available, for more favorable terms of distribution. The amount which it is physically possible for them to gain by this means is quite limited. How much would their wages be increased if they could secure all that now goes to employers? Induce capitalists to loan their money and give their best skill and energy in management for nothing, and how much would thereby be added to the general sum of wages? The data are not at hand for an exact answer; but a calculation lately made on the basis of the figures of the last census would seem to indicate that profits and interest amount to about one half as much as wages, and that a distribution that should leave to the employer nothing, would, at the most, increase wages but fifty per cent.

Now it is obvious that no class of men will or can furnish capital and expend skill and energy for nothing. It is safe to assert that the average employer would close his business were his own returns reduced to one half of their present rate. An increase of one quarter in total wages would, then, seem to be the utmost that is to be hoped for under present conditions. Now if the strikes that aim to bring about this re-adjustment lessen production, they farther reduce the available margin on which the workmen are trying to draw. If an increase of twenty-five cents on the dollar is all that can be hoped for while the productiveness of industry is unchanged, a very limited increase is all that can be had if industries are deranged and their productiveness lessened. It must be by better means than strikes that any considerable gain is ever to be realized by workmen.

Coöperation aims to increase the margin from which the increment of gain is to be drawn. It makes industry more productive; it gives to the employer some-what more, and to the laborer much more than they now receive. Its moral advantage over the present sys-tem is greater than its material one, since it settles questions of division in a manner so obviously just as to hold all conflicting claims in abeyance. It destroys the material out of which contests are made.

The key to the question as to what system ought to emerge from the present chaotic condition of industry is found in the fact that employers and workmen sustain to each other two distinct relations, of which one is antago-nistic and the other harmonious. In merely dividing the product of industry their interests conflict; in creating it they are in perfect harmony. Competition and even arbitration bring into prominence the relation which develops conflict; coöperation brings into sole view the relation tending to unity.

We used constantly to be told, and still frequently hear, that no intelligent conflict between capitalists and laborers is possible; that their interests are completely identical, and that their normal relation is one of para-disaical harmony. Frequently as this statement was formerly reiterated, the laborers were not convinced; and, in the meanwhile, the practical relation between them and their employers grew constantly less para-disaical. There is, in prevalent discussions, a confusion of thought which an analysis of actual relations ought easily to remove.

We have said that there is harmony of interest between the two industrial classes in the operation of production, and diversity of interest in the operation of distribution. Under a wage system the effect of this twofold relation is to create a conflict, and at the same time to set limits to the overt acts to which the conflict might lead. So long as this system continues, the utmost that is to be hoped from education is that the limitations may be applied wisely. Capitalists and laborers are interested that as much wealth as possible shall be produced, for both are dependent on the product. The mill must be run, or neither owner nor employé can receive anything. When, however, the product is realized, the relation changes; the question is now one of mere division. The more there is for the owner, the less can go to the men; and no education can remove this source of conflict.

The crew of a whaling ship are paid, as we shall later notice, by shares of the cargo; and if the proportion to be received by each man were not settled in advance by contract, they would naturally work with good will until the cargo should be brought into port, and then develop a hopeless wrangle over the division of it. They would not, however, go to the length of burning the ship, since all would need it for future use; but would they delay the refitting of it? Would they attempt to enlarge their returns, at the cost of the owner, to an extent that would prevent him from building more ships? Here is the field in which intelligence may do its work. Ignorance and passion make the limits of overt action broad, and tolerate much that discourages production, and even lessens the store of wealth accumulated. Intelligence narrows the field of strife, suppresses all violence, and confines within a minimum range all measures which reduce the product of industry; but within the limits as ultimately set, it allows the conflict to continue.

For clearness of illustration a case has been selected in which production and distribution are separated in time; whalers first secure the oil, and then divide it. In most industries the two processes go on together; wealth is divided day by day, and week by week, as it is produced, and the relation of employers and employed is, therefore, not an alternation in time, from a condition in which their relations harmonize to one in which they antagonize, but presents a permanent harmony in one respect, and a permanent antagonism in another. Both parties are interested in continued and successful production; but in the mere matter of distribution their antagonism is as permanent as their connection. To ignore either side of the relation is unintelligent. If it be incendiary to proclaim an irrepressible conflict between capital and labor, it is imbecile to reiterate that there is no possible ground of conflict between them, and that the contests which actually occur, are the fruit of ignorance.

While there is no such thing as changing the mode
of dividing a common possession in such a manner as to
give one partner more without giving the other less,
there is such a thing as making the plan of division so
obviously just, as to settle once for all the question of
proportionate shares, and to concentrate the energies of
all on the securing of a large product. Put the parties
who create wealth on such a footing that neither can
claim more than he gets, without violating an obvious
principle of equity, and they will make the division un-
thinkingly, and plan and work only for benefits which
accrue alike to all.

Such is the aim of coöperation. It is the principle
of solidarity in a new field. The great consolidations
now in process are for belligerent ends; this is for an
amicable end. The organization of capital, on the one
hand, and that of labor, on the other, enable these
agents to fight a good battle over the division of products; coöperation allays strife, and enables them to
expend their whole energy in creating products. Re-
curring again to the diagram which illustrates the process of distribution, we find that present consolidations
are taking place between the horizontal lines, while
coöperation always crosses a line, and merges two
classes which are now in a hostile attitude.

This blending of classes is the feature even of that
partial coöperation, known as profit-sharing. The workman does not, by this plan, own capital and receive in-

terest; but he uses it, and receives a share of net profits.
He is not a capitalist, but he is an *entrepreneur*, or employer; and the benefit derived from the system, consists in the fact that he performs his part of the direc-
tive function exceedingly well. All the workmen with
their employers constitute, collectively, an exceptionally
good *entrepreneur*.

Mr. Mill's illustrations of this system, taken from the
workshops of Paris, are familiar, as are the instances
of the Paris and Orleans railroad, and the Whitwood
collieries described by Mr. Sedley Taylor. The Labor
Report of Massachusetts for 1886 shows that profit-
sharing has, for some time, had a foothold in this State.
The introduction of the system into new fields has, of
late, been of almost daily occurrence. The success
already attained places this mode of industry beyond
the limit of schemes which can claim only a theoretical
support. It is, indeed, essentially right, and ought to
succeed; but it also has succeeded.

An illustration of profit-sharing which is near at
hand and brilliantly successful is afforded by the whale
fishery of New England. This industry places in a
conspicuous light the basis of the success of the system,
namely, the increase in production which attends it.

The difference between the product of interested
labor and that of labor which is careless and lazy is
always noticeable; but in the whale fishery it is exceptionally great. An eager search, a zealous pursuit and

a resolute attack are secured only by the stimulus of a
personal interest in the result. Superintendence by
owners is impossible, unless the captain be a proprie-
tor; and if he is so, the plan becomes, to that extent,
coöperative. Even though the captain were the sole
owner, his best efforts would not ensure a profitable
voyage, unless a heartier obedience could be secured
than is usually seen on ships. Moreover payment by
the day might interest the crew in unduly prolonging
the voyage. Profit-sharing has, therefore, driven the
wage system from this industry. A summary of results
attained by this method in other fields shows that the
same basis of success exists elsewhere, though not
often in the same degree. Profit-sharing, as a rule,
secures interested and successful efforts, increases the
product to be divided, and while giving to the capitalist
somewhat more, gives to the laborer much more than
can be had under the present plan of eternal belligerency.

It is an advantage of the system of profit-sharing that
it may be gradually developed. It may differ at first
from the wage system by a small gradation, which may
be increased by successive changes. The prevailing
rate of wages may be paid, and a small proportion of
the net profits may be added, as a bonus, in the case of
a few workmen in responsible positions. The amount
distributed and the number of the recipients may be
gradually increased, until the amount received from

this source constitutes a main dependence of every workman. Then only is the laborer so far merged in the employer as to secure the maximum benefit from the relation.

Profit-sharing, when fully developed, requires that a provision be made for unprofitable years by a reserve fund, from which, when profits for the time disappear, the stipend necessary for the laborer's maintenance may be drawn.

It is to be noted as theoretically possible that, in industries conducted on the share principle, disputes may arise concerning the size of the shares. The seamen on a whaling-ship who receive each a two-hundredth part of the cargo may strike for the one-hundred-and-fiftieth. Strikes of this kind do not, in fact, occur, doubtless because the workmen realize the more adequate justice which is done to them by the share system, and are unwilling to disturb its successful operation.

The increased willingness of employers to adopt this system, in some of its gradations, is a noteworthy fact of the present period. Four systems of industrial organization are now on trial, with a prospect that the fittest will, in the end, survive. If the competitive system in its degenerate state leads to strikes and lockouts, arbitration will survive as between these two. If arbitration concentrates the attention too much on the mere division of the product, profit-sharing may outlive it. If profit-sharing still leaves as subject for dispute the proportion of profits to be given to labor, full coöperation may, in many fields, be the ultimate survivor.

A better mode of industrial organization replaces a worse, as a better mechanical process replaces an inferior one, by enabling those who use it to undersell their competitors. The immediate effect of the adoption of profit-sharing by a few establishments is to increase the reward of the laborers employed in them. This, of itself, is a powerful incentive to other workmen in the same occupation to strive to secure a like increase. If this leads to strikes, it gives to the profit-sharing establishment a relative advantage, in addition to that which is inherent in the plan itself. An employer whose working force may always be depended on may undersell one whose men are watching for opportunities to increase their wages by a strike. Under present conditions profit-sharing must, in order to survive in the struggle of systems, prove superior, not to competition working smoothly and successfully, but to competition essentially vitiated and subject to incessant friction. It is safe to assert that the plan of profit-sharing is inherently capable of doing this. In some fields it has proved superior to competition at its best; it will easily excel, in many more fields, the wreck of the old system with which it is now brought into comparison.

If a corporation were to adopt the share system in dealing with its employés, and were to pay the amount given to them, in excess of daily wages, in the form of stock, the effect would be to gradually transmute the partial coöperation into the complete form. New establishments started on this plan have, as a rule, perished in their infancy. Experience has shown that the mortality among them is increased by loans of capital made to them either by governments or by philanthropic societies. Such loans strain the enterprises at their weakest point, namely, their general management. Profit-sharing retains the experienced employer as the general director, and enlists the interest of every workman in the oversight of details within his province. Full coöperation, unless established by the gradual method above spoken of, renders a managing committee necessary, and the inexperience of the men selected for this function imperils the enterprise. A loan increases this danger, by increasing the scale of operations undertaken, and by causing the enterprise to start under a burden of debt. Great as are the disadvantages of small production, a coöperative experiment has the best chance of success when it submits to them, and acquires the needed experience as it enlarges its operations.

The survival of full coöperation, in the long rivalry of systems, depends on its power to excel other systems in the results which it ultimately yields. Failures at the outset may deter experiments in this direction, and make the introduction of this method proceed slowly; but they do not change the law of survival. That is a question, not of initial risks, but of results gained by the successful experiment. If one cotton mill run on the coöperative plan shall ever surpass other mills in economy of production, to an extent that will enable it to undersell their product in the market, it may ultimately compel them to adopt this method, though a score of earlier experiments have failed.

The new political economy must recognize, as one of its principles, this special and higher competition by which systems are tested. Individual competition, the basis of the traditional science, is, in extensive fields, a thing of the past. It has been vitiated by combinations, leaving society without its former regulative principle. Yet is is only temporarily that wages are to be adjusted by a crude struggle of labor unions with employers' associations; the permanent mode of adjustment must be by some application of moral force. Arbitration, profit-sharing and full coöperation depart radically from the old competitive method, and appeal, each in its own way, to principles of equity, in dividing the proceeds of industry. Yet among the systems as such competition should rule, in determining which is fittest for ultimate survival. Coöperation will, by this process, have a fair chance in the industrial world. If, in the comparison with other systems, it is shown that it ought to survive, it will do so, and that regardless of initial failures.

The chaotic condition of industrial society opens wider than it was ever opened before the door for new forms of organization. As the easiest of adoption, the plan of adjusting wages by arbitration bids fair to make the most rapid headway. When thus renovated, the wage system will bear a far better comparison with the two coöperative methods, and will have, by so much, a better chance of surviving. In some large fields it may continue indefinitely. The comparison between it and the coöperative systems has yet to be made by the tests of the market. A practical comparison of the relative merits of profit-sharing and full coöperation, is still farther in the future. On general principles that system should come earliest which best adapts itself to an imperfect condition of society; and those forms should come later which are the expression of a higher development. On these grounds, which are not wholly speculative, the two systems which are based on the fraternal principle of partnership, may be expected to survive those which are based on a principle of strife.

There are certain establishments nominally coöperative which have little significance, as bearing on the labor question. The chief of these is the Rochdale form of the coöperative store. Workmen variously employed contribute capital, hire men of their own class as managers, sell goods for cash at market prices, pay a fixed percentage per annum to the share-holders, and divide the remaining profits among the customers, on a *pro rata* plan, according to the amount of their purchases. The essential principle of true coöperation is

its obliteration of dividing lines in industrial society.
Workmen become, by means of it, employers of their
own labor, and distribution, the cause of strife, is conducted on a new plan. To this result the Rochdale enterprise contributes nothing. The men who own the
store remain, as wage workers, in the mills; and the
division of the product of their own industry proceeds
according to the old plan, and with the same liability
to conflict as if the store had never existed. Yet,
by a strange perversity of nomenclature, this process
has been termed "coöperative distribution," apparently
because the store distributes useful articles among the
members of the community who patronize it. The industry conducted in it is the ordinary mercantile one
of buying in bulk and selling in detail; and it creates
the various utilities which we have analyzed as the result of the merchant's function. It is productive in as
complete a sense of the term as the spinning of wool or
the raising of sheep. To term the process "distribution" is to increase the difficulty which besets the student of grasping the essential nature of the distributive
process. This is a division of the abstract value created
by industry, not a carrying of parcels to and fro in
express wagons.

Whatever the Rochdale process is, it is not distributive, since it leaves the men who own it still working
for wages under their old employers. In the case even
of the managers and clerks in the store itself the wage

system survives; these men are paid for their services like the clerks of any merchant. The process
is complex, and, in reality, is only quasi-coöperative.
It may, perhaps, be termed mixed coöperation, since
the essential peculiarity of it is that men who are employés in one industry become proprietors in another.
There is a union of capital and labor in the same hands,
but not in the same industry. The store is of value to
the customers which it serves, since it offers to them a
virtual reduction of prices, and at the same time presents the savings thus effected in periodical dividends,
which the receivers are encouraged to invest as capital
in the enterprise. It has an invaluable educating effect
upon the men who maintain it. It also reacts favorably
upon the character of the mercantile class, since it impels all who would hold their own in competition with
it to sell honest goods at fair prices. It is a valuable
social institution; but it leaves the labor problem where
it found it.

There has existed, in the case of the English coöperative stores, elements of success which are not to be
found in this country. There was, at the outset, a lack
of retail shops that were either good or cheap. There
was an abnormal extension of the credit system among
dealers; and there was an absence among them of that
sharply competitive spirit which leads merchants to
strive to outdo each other in reducing prices to a minimum. There was a large homogeneous population of

manufacturing employés, well organized, and specially imbued with the teachings of Robert Owen. The association, therefore, had exceptional material in its members, and an unusual field for securing custom by the virtual reduction of prices which it was able to offer. That similar experiments have been less successful in this country is, in part, due to the fact that they are less needed. The absence of the conditions of success signifies the presence of conditions in which the work of the store may be done by other agencies, and in which more important fields are offering for coöperative enterprise.

Competition is here sharper, and retail shops are better than in England; it is, therefore, less easy for a store established on the new plan to attract customers. If, in any locality, this is not true, it is an evidence that, in this one respect, the local conditions make a coöperative store both desirable and practicable; and if the other conditions are favorable, such an enterprise should be started. If inertness on the part of workmen retards it, there is a field for moral influence to do its work.

Complete coöperation has succeeded on the largest scale in agriculture. The economic motive for this mode of living is less urgent in this department of industry than in others. Agriculture is not yet centralized, as are manufactures, and the relations of the classes engaged in it are not strained to a dangerous

extent.   Yet success in coöperative farming is comparatively easy; and wherever a special motive impels men
to this mode of living, a community may be founded
and made to thrive.   Such an extra-economic motive
may be afforded by religion.   The Shakers, the Amana
Communists, the Perfectionists and others have been
united by bonds other than those of pecuniary interest.
Such communities are exceptional, and, like the coöperative stores, contribute little toward the solution
of the labor question.   Their success is valuable, not
mainly as a proof that agricultural communism is, in a
local way, possible, but as an evidence that this mode
of living is favorable, as it appears to have been at
Jerusalem of old, to religious brotherhood among men.
The early Christian commune was a success spiritually,
if not otherwise; and if a village on the communal plan
can, here and there, be made to thrive economically and
religiously, it may contribute its little share toward
promoting the growth of fraternal feeling among those
who look upon it from the outer world.   As in the case
of the Rochdale enterprise, its chief service to society is
educational.

A motive of a directly opposite kind may induce a
large city to adopt measures tending in a communistic
direction.   The city may make a complete surrender
to its mercantile environment.   It may conclude that
it has more in common with the business corporation
than with the state as a political entity, and that it can

best promote the comfort of its inhabitants by owning gas and water works and street railways, and endeavoring to manage them in the interest of all. If it succeeds in such a course the fact is due to the strictly local patronage of the business enterprises undertaken. The city does not, thereby, cater to the general outside public, and it therefore comes into no competition with private producers, whose better management would bring their municipal rival to failure. Such public enterprises are, in a sense, coöperative, since all who pay taxes are share-holders in them; but they throw no light on the relations of capital and labor. Their work lies in the department of municipal finance.

Prison industry conducted on "public account" is a useful form of coöperation. The socialistic ideal is realized in a great reformatory managed on this plan; there is "labor applied to public resources," and there is strict equity in the division of the proceeds. In such an establishment all the profits and more go to the laborers. Yet motives of immediate economy favor the letting of prison labor to contractors; and if the plan of working on state account shall ultimately prevail, it will be because of the opportunity which it affords of effecting the moral reformation of the prisoners. Against such a gain no good government would weigh for a moment the petty economy to be effected by other methods. Good government is, unhappily, not among the data of our own present calculations, and the contract system may be an available compromise of interests; yet if our state governments improve, they may be expected to favor more and more the system which gives the best moral results. Since, then, the coöperative form of prison industry has other than economic ends in view, it sheds no light on the labor problem.

Public work-houses for tramps would be a natural adjunct of a reformatory system, and would help to dissociate the tramp question from the general labor problem. It would intercept anarchism near its source, and relieve the municipalities, on the one hand, and the labor organizations on the other. In so far as this measure would clear the market of men whose presence depresses wages, it would contribute indirectly toward improving the workmen's condition. It would not otherwise affect the mode of distributing wealth. If the great combinations now forming shall end by filling the market with idle men, such measures as this will have a new importance.

Upon arbitration, profit-sharing, and full coöperation must be our dependence for the solution of the labor problem. These measures are named in the direct order of their availability, and in the reverse order of their intrinsic excellence. Arbitration is the easiest, and will doubtless have, in the decades immediately coming, the greatest extension. It is, however, only the more radical measures, those which merge classes now hostile, that can insure a reign of permanent peace in the industrial world. Profit-sharing makes the workman, in a sense, an employer; and full coöperation makes him both an employer and a capitalist. In neither relation is he a disturbing element, for in neither can he well fail to receive obvious justice.

The question which of the three modes of adjusting the rewards of labor shall ultimately prevail is to be determined, not by the comparative difficulty of the methods, but, as already shown, by their comparative excellence when they prove successful. Original failures count for little, and the result of one successful experiment counts for much, in deciding the question of ultimate survival. That system will, in each particular field, survive and continue which, in that field, is permanently the best. As different fields offer different conditions, it is improbable that any one method of industry will become universal. The three general systems may continue, each in the field to which it is specially adapted.

The value of coöperation, partial or complete, is not limited to its effect on the men who directly participate in its benefits. A few coöperative establishments react on the condition of men who still work for wages; and this effect must become more marked as the system of arbitration shall obtain a foothold. Tribunals for adjusting wages will need a standard of justice, in making their awards. At first they may proceed blindly, striving only to effect a rude compromise of opposing claims. They may "split differences," and content themselves if they thereby avert strikes and allow business to continue. Where the rate is a dollar, and the workmen claim a dollar and a half, they may give a dollar and a quarter. This would be a welcome escape from the present chaos, but it would not be arbitration of a highly developed form.

In the end there must be standards of equity in the division of the products of industry. Certain proportions of a gross return will come to be recognized as a rightful reward of employers and of employed. The proportions will vary in different fields; but if, in any field, a few profit-sharing establishments exist and yield good results, they will assist in setting the standard to which arbitration will conform. The rewards of labor under the wage system may thus be, in a measure, gauged by those which are realized under the system of shares. Profit-sharing, even on a limited scale, may diffuse benefits over the whole industrial field.

The coöperative principle in its different forms is the Christian socialism of Maurice, Kingsley, Hughes, and their worthy co-laborers. It meets an imperative human need, and must grow surely, though not, as reformers are wont to estimate progress, rapidly. Time is requisite for the development of its completer forms; and if arbitration can tide over the interval of transition, and secure outward peace until the conditions of

true fraternity mature, it will effect, by its indirect results, the redemption of society.

The condition of success in any general system of
coöperation is mental and moral progress.   The permanence of republics has long been known to depend on
these conditions; they are short lived when the people
are ignorant or bad.   Christian socialism is economic
republicanism; and it can come no sooner, stay no
longer, and rise, in quality, no higher than intelligence
and virtue among the people.

It is only step by step that we can hope to approach
the social ideal that is beginning to reveal itself.   Im-
patience at the conditions of natural progress is the
root of political socialism.   A few men have had vis-
ions of an ideal state, not indeed the one which will
exist in reality, when the better tendencies now at
work shall be consummated, but an imaginary condition in which countries shall become workshops under
political control.   Men are to be found possessing the
infinite wisdom and virtue necessary for directing such
operations as must be undertaken, and, by a greater
miracle, these men, when found, are to be placed in
power and kept there by popular elections.   Human
imperfections are a forgotten fact in the situation.

The socialistic state would destroy personal freedom.
It might be practicable, if men were morally perfect;
but it would be intolerable.   Men will not want it in
the millennium, and they cannot have it earlier.   The

socialist does not propose to wait for the development of a perfect moral state before realizing his dream. Evolution is slow, and manufacture rapid; he will, therefore, make the ideal state with his own hands. He will plan it, and secure the popular decree that shall put it into operation. "Let there be socialism;" and there will be socialism — over night, possibly: anarchy will put an end to the experiment in the morning.

Viewed on but one side the socialistic ideal has a beauty that captivates the intellect which fairly grasps it. It bursts on the view like an Italian landscape from the summit of an Alpine pass, and lures men over the fatal declivity. Individualism appears to say, "Here is the world; take, every one, what you can get of it. Not too violently, not altogether unjustly; but with this limitation, selfishly, let every man make his possessions as large as he may. For the strong there is much, and for his children more; for the weak there is little, and for his children less."

Socialism appears to say, "Here is the world; take it as a family domain. Enjoy it as children, each according to his needs; labor as brethren, each according to his strength. Let justice supplant might in the distribution, so that, when there is abundance, all may participate, and when there is scarcity, all may share in the self-denial. If there is loss of independence, there will be gain of interdependence; he who thinks less for himself, will be forced to think more for his brother.

If there is loss of brute force gained in the rude struggle of competition, there is gain of moral power acquired by the interchange of kindly offices. The beautiful bond which scientists term altruism will bind the human family together as no other tie can bind them."

Sufferers under an actual system naturally look for deliverance and for a deliverer. The impression has prevailed among working men, that a new device of some kind might free them from their difficulties. Ideal socialism seems to meet this expectation, and those who preach it as a practical aim, naturally receive a hearing. The way in which the old system is defended is often as repulsive as the new system is attractive. When one teacher bids the poor submit, and another bids them hope, they will not be long in choosing between them. Yet there is no royal road to general comfort. There is much to be gained by studying the changes which are actually in progress, but nothing by inventing artificial schemes of society. The new dispensation is coming, but not with observation; and it has no particular apostles. Very substantial have been the gains of recent years; and in the promise of the future there may already be discerned an ideal surpassing, in its attractiveness, the socialistic dream. It preserves, what socialism from the outset sacrifices, freedom. By steps which are never retraced society is drawing nearer to it; and the ideal itself is valuable, not indeed as something to be grasped by a frantic effort, but as a means of lightening, by intelligent hope, the steps by which mankind are destined to approach it.

CHAPTER XI.

COMPETITION is no longer adequate to account for the phenomena of social industry. What was once assumed as a universal law is now but partial in its operation. Economic science needs modernizing; it was a half-century after the publication of the *Wealth of Nations* that the earlier railroads were built, and it was a century after its publication that the great railway and telegraph monopolies were effected. During that century the economic activities of the world have gained, in intensity, more than they had done during the entire antecedent period of recorded history. Diversity of products, rapidity of exchanges and industrial organization are the criteria; and if we compare the condition, in these respects, of early Oriental monarchies with the condition of the world in 1776, and that, again, with its present state, we shall find the second difference greater than the first. Steam and electricity, migrations and inventions, have brought this about. Economic theories adapted to a civilization midway in its development cannot apply equally well to a civilization at its present maximum. We need an economic science adapted to steam, or, more accurately, to an intensified social activity. The system of Adam Smith has advanced, but not sufficiently; and what is lacking is more than the trivial adaptations sometimes attempted; it is undetected principles.

There is something deeper than competition in the economic life of men; and the relation of competition to the underlying law has not been analyzed. The principle whereby the struggle of many men, each for himself, to secure wealth is made to work out the general good of all, has all the beauty that is claimed for it. We have noticed, however, in an earlier chapter, the moral limitations that hedge about this struggle. The contest is never unrestricted. A Spirit of Justice is ever standing over the contestants, and bidding them compete only thus and thus. This they may do; that they may not do; and the prohibitions increase with time. Competition at best exists by sufferance, and the power that tolerates and controls it is moral.

We have now to notice a still more decisive manner in which the moral sovereignty asserts itself. It not only regulates competition in its modes, but, at will, it thrusts the whole process aside. It is because there have long been departments of practical economy not left to competition, that there has always been, in science, some need of a province of non-competitive economics. It is because these activities are increasing apace with the rapid developments of the past century, that the need is now pressing.

We have seen that the ultimate end of political economy is not, as is generally assumed, the mere quantitative increase of wealth. Society, as an organic unit, has a higher economic end. That end is the attainment of the greatest quantity, the highest quality, and the most just distribution of wealth. It is the true subjection of matter, the placing of it in the most rational condition, absolute and relative. The matter and force of external nature are to be brought into that state which, in itself, is best, and they are to be brought into that relation of ownership which best promotes the general happiness. Matter modified by labor in accordance with enlightened reason may be termed rational wealth; it is this that society is pursuing, and partially realizing.

The actual wealth of society varies more or less from the ideal standard, and is but partly rational. Much of it is not of high quality, and much that is so is not well distributed; it is but partly beneficent, in itself, and in its relation to owners. Immoral books, poisonous beverages, and adulterated articles of food are wealth of an actual but irrational sort; so also are all things that minister to vice. These are real commodities, because, somewhere in society, are men whose impulses crave them; they are irrational, because the reason that is inherent in society as a whole does not want them, and would cast them out if it could.

The want of a true teleology, the failure to discover

the τέλος, or ultimate goal of social tendencies, and the consequent failure to discriminate between actual and rational wealth, does not, indeed, deprive current political economy of its practical value; but it lessens that value, and throws the system more and more out of harmony with the modern spirit. A little while hence, and the omission will be disastrous.

The competitive mode of production and distribution has been adopted by society because, in its day, it has given the nearest practical approximation to the standard of rational wealth. Imperfect as are its results, those of any other system would have been more imperfect; they would have rendered the wealth of society less, worse, or worse distributed. As compared with them, the principle of competition has increased, improved, and with rude equity divided the products of industry; and for this reason only has it been tolerated.

The vast residuum of competition which still exists continues to do a similar work, and owes to this fact its prospect of survival. Inherently it has no vitality; it needs and possesses a *raison d'être*, and, in the absence of it, would cease to exist. It rests on moral law. In the department of distribution its working may be less perfect than in that of production. It may be but a spontaneous and imperfect agent for dividing wealth, with approximate justice, among the members of society; yet it is only because it serves this purpose, and so long as it does so, that it is tolerated; and there

never was a time when it would not have been thrust aside, could society have seen its way to the adoption of another method which would more nearly have realized the rational end in view. Powerful as the competitive principle appears in practice, it is not supreme, still less, self-existent; it is the creature of an exigency, created as the rude servant of a higher power, and continuing by sufferance. It is perpetually on trial, and its minutest acts are subject to the scrutiny of that supreme moral court to whose verdict all systems, economic as well as civil and legal, must submit.

Society does not and will not completely abandon the competitive principle ; it is still needed as an agent of distribution, and it is the sole means on which we can rely for the securing of a large product to distribute. Yet, if what we have claimed be true, society should hold this agent in abeyance within limited fields of industry, whenever, within those limits, a better system is available. This it actually does. Sometimes, as in railroad operations, competition works sluggishly, interruptedly, or not at all; sometimes, as in the transactions of labor and capital, it works, for a time, one-sidedly and cruelly, and then almost ceases to do its work. It may happen that, in exactly that field in which competition operates unusually ill, another method may operate especially well, and the comparison of results may be in favor of the latter. If once society becomes conscious that this is the fact, farewell to one particular form of competition.

That the future field of non-competitive economics will be vast is less surprising than that its present field is considerable. Arbitration promises to replace the former agent of distribution in a comprehensive way. Coöperation is the antithesis of competition; wherever it exists the competitive struggle is held, to some extent, in abeyance. In practice coöperation is most frequently of an incomplete kind, and a greater or less residuum of competition remains; but any realization of the one principle means the elimination of somewhat of the other; and, moreover, whatever is done by a public or governmental agency is done, in a sense, coöperatively. What we have now to consider is a certain displacement of competition which is of long standing, and which, therefore, serves to show that society has always been ready to set the process aside, whenever it has been able, by other means, to better attain the rational end which it has had in view.

It is the misfortune of the narrow and illogical definitions of wealth formerly current, and not yet entirely abandoned, to exclude from their classification much that is really wealth; and the excluded portion is, to a great extent, of the highest and most rational quality. It embodies itself often in tenuous and unsubstantial matter, as in the vibrating particles that constitute light and sound; but it ministers to the highest wants of human nature, and is tributary to true and permanent happiness. As we formerly endeavored to show, these finer commodities are to the soul what those of the grosser sort are to the body; and if man is dependent on literal bread for life, he is dependent on loaves of a more spiritual sort for a life that is worth the living.

Now these most rational forms of wealth have regularly been distributed on more or less communistic principles. Beauty and truth have never been monopolized and sold to the highest bidder. Public agencies have embodied them in the delicate material forms that come within our definition of wealth, and have distributed them freely to all, as the Roman emperors distributed the corn of Egypt. Not that all such commodities have been so distributed; the competitions of the market have determined the ownership of some of the costliest of them. There has been an interesting intermingling of coöperative and competitive action in this department, and it will be instructive to ascertain the limits where the one process ceases and the other begins.

From the days of Athens until now the best products of art have been, under one or another form of procedure, purchased by the public and assigned to the general use. Statues by the Greek masters were in temples or on the street. The greatest architectural works of the Romans were public theatres, baths, basilicas, fora, and temples. The early Christian community, a state within a state, expended its best efforts in the adornment of churches; and the triumphs of the Renaissance were in works of this kind. Most of the works of the great masters are now free for the enjoyment of all.

Yet, from the first, also, many products of art have been sold in the open market and purchased for private use. Wealthy men have always, whether from taste, vanity or both, been consumers of artistic products. The amount of this consumption was small in Greece, larger in Rome, small again in the early Christian state, and even at the period of the Renaissance, but is increasingly large in recent times. The accumulation of vast fortunes in our own country may be expected to increase this tendency; while the frequent gift or bequest of private fortunes for purposes of public benefit may be expected to proportionately increase the amount of such products placed at the free disposal of the people. This is one regal function of the money king. Rational wealth in æsthetic form is, in great part, owned and enjoyed non-competitively.

This free disbursal of valuable products is distribution of an extraordinary kind; and, singularly enough, it in no way changes the relation of employers to the employed. Competition is, by this means, suppressed only among the consumers of particular articles; the industrial groups which produce them are not affected. Artists strive to excel each other in the quality of their work, and receive for it the price determined in the open market by ordinary laws. This producing group receives its share of the general wealth of society in the same manner as others, and subdivides it among its individual members in the same way. The artist must pay his assistants the market price for their labor. The supplanting of competition consists in the fact that other groups get works of art without being obliged to buy them, and to bid against each other in securing them. Society pays for the products which it thus disburses from the proceeds of taxes; and, as these are gauged more or less according to the property of the persons who pay them, while the products purchased by the means are placed at the free disposal of all, it would seem that, here at least, men realized the socialistic ideal, producing according to their ability, and consuming according to their need.

Yet the consumption of such products is gauged, not by general need, but by inclination and opportunity; and in this difference lies the basis of the system of disbursing rational wealth. Were competition to determine the amount which each person might enjoy of these fine and costly products, the poor would get none of them; and, in accordance with the law cited in an earlier chapter, they would lose their desire for them. This would involve a personal deterioration; and it is this which the state interposes to prevent. For its own reasons it determines that men shall not thus degenerate; that they shall be educated to desire and to use the refining products of the artist's labor. The ultimate purpose is non-economic; it is to elevate the nature of individual men, and to make the state sounder and safer. Yet the process contributes to the economic end of society; it enables men to advance directly toward the *summum bonum* of industrial action. It keeps alive the popular demand for works of art, and insures the continued production and consumption of many of the better forms of wealth.

Commodities which minister to the desire for knowledge come next in order, in the extent to which they have been disbursed at public expense. Oral instruction has not always been free, and books have been so still less frequently. In the later ages of the world, however, schools of some sort have been cheap enough for all but the very destitute, and this cheapness has been the result of some form of public action. Commodities embodying knowledge have been either given to consumers or sold to them for less than their cost. The mediæval church assumed this governmental function among others. The modern public school is either entirely free or so nearly so as to throw its chief cost upon the State, and open it to universal use.

Endowments may be regarded as being, originally, gifts to the public, though administered without official intervention; and schools established on this basis are not, as far as the enjoyment of their products is concerned, to be separated, in principle, from other public agencies for producing and disbursing those commodities which are food for the intellect. The endowed colleges of England and America are, in their effect on students, public institutions. While these agencies are distributing oral instruction in a manner more or less independent of competition, free libraries, endowed or otherwise, are doing the same for the more substantial instruments of education. Here again there is an ulterior end in view; the welfare of citizens and the safety of the State demand the free disbursal of these products. Yet the economic effect of the process is real and important, and public instruction demands consideration from the economist, as well as from the educator and the statesman. Rational wealth in the forms that nourish the intellect is, to a great extent, distributed non-competitively.

There are times when the Church is to be regarded as one of the departments of the State; the material appliances of religion then fall in the same category as those of education and artistic culture. The State for ages nourished the heart as well as the taste and the intellect. The peculiarity of modern times and of our own country is the discontinuance of this process. In America, State and Church have separated; and, while the State retains the instruments of instruction, and, to a great extent, those of æsthetic culture, it has thrown the distribution of religious nutriment back into the market.

It feeds the intellect and the taste, but leaves the heart, like the body, to be nourished by each man for himself. Yet the necessities of the case have not admitted of free individual action in this department. Men cannot obtain the needed sustenance separately, and voluntary coöperation has at once assumed the function abandoned by the State. Churches are the best established of coöperative societies, and their economic functions are a fascinating subject of the non-competitive division of political economy.

In a few countries governmental coöperation is extended over the field of railway transportation; and that the same will, ultimately, be the case in America is the belief of some persons who realize the evils of railroad combinations, but fail to see the good which comes from such competition as still exists in this department. Pools do not prevent companies from striving to surpass each other in perfecting their methods, and in securing, by efficient management, a large production of wealth. Here, under a *régime* of fixed rates for transportation, lies their sole chance of increasing their profits.

The incentive to a state management of railroads is, in principle, identical with that which prompts to the forms of non-competitive action already noticed. The object is to insure the production and disbursement of forms of wealth which are essential to the public welfare. It is not, however, the regular products of railway operations that are concerned, but certain special products, the study of which will reveal an important and, as yet, unanalyzed economic principle, which we may term that of inappropriable utilities.

Labor imparts utilities to matter, and the impulse to it is that these may be enjoyed by the laborer. To be enjoyed they must be owned; the fruits that the laborer raises or the implements that he fashions must belong to him, and to no other person. It is the nature of some utilities to be taken completely into the possession of him who produces them. Others, however, elude him. It is the nature of certain utilities to flee from him who creates them, and diffuse themselves among the members of the community. The builder of a house is able to appropriate the greater portion of the utility created. The roof shelters and the walls enclose that which makes his life enjoyable. If the house be comely in form, and attractive in surroundings, he has the most constant enjoyment of its beauty. Yet this enjoyment cannot be monopolized; the tasteful exterior of the dwelling, with the beauty of its shade-trees and lawn, create an inappropriable utility which distributes itself among neighboring proprietors. Its presence is indicated, and its measure expressed, by the increased price of adjoining property.

In the case of railroads the inappropriable utilities are so great as almost to overbalance those which can be retained by the owners. The railroad creates a

value far in excess of that which its projectors can
realize; and this distributes itself among the adjacent
population, and appears in the enhanced value of lands
and the increased rewards of general industry. It has
often happened that a railroad which enriched the population of the section which it traversed, rendered its
projectors bankrupt.

The granting of public aid to railroad companies is a
recognition of the principle of inappropriable utilities;
it is a payment, by the public, for a value which the
company is compelled to transfer to it from sheer inability to retain it for itself. The land grant is a crude
mode of effecting this payment, which has very properly
been discontinued because of the abuses which it has
entailed. The values created attach in part to the
lands granted to the company, and in part to the alter-
nate sections which, by the practice of our government,
have been reserved for itself. The public and the company thus share equally in this particular benefit.

Much of the utility created by the building and
operation of the railroad remains inappropriable. The
important fact is, that this portion becomes a matter of
indifference to the corporation. Benefits which the railroad company confers, but for which it can secure no
reward, are of no consequence to it; they may, therefore, be sacrificed with impunity. Through the working of this principle of inappropriable utilities, much of
the welfare of large populations is intrusted to corpo-

rations having no interest in maintaining it. It will be subserved as long as the company has nothing to gain by sacrificing it, not longer.

Recently, in our country, the company or its managers have often had something to gain by sacrificing the welfare of the inhabitants of the districts through which they pass. Discriminating rates for transportation, as well as other abuses, have recklessly made or marred the welfare of sections of the country. The State is involved in this; it has an interest in the elusive but real utilities which a railroad, properly managed, scatters throughout a land. Can it best secure them by supervising the railways or by owning them? Experience thus far strongly favors the former alternative, as both more profitable and more safe. That which places the regulating and the owning of railroads by the state in the same category with public education is the fact that in both cases does a public agency intervene in order to secure the general diffusion of important utilities.

It is evident that the principle of inappropriable utilities is applicable to every form of industry in which the community has an independent interest, and in especial to those of an educational and religious character. The exemption of institutions of this kind from taxation is a partial refunding of the value diffused by them through the community.

There is, then, a province of economics not ordinarily

recognized, because wholly or partially outside of the range of competition. The province has long been a considerable one, and the changes now in progress, the development of the system of arbitration and of that of coöperation, will ultimately give to it a vastly greater extension. A portion of it has failed to receive attention from economists in consequence of illogical conceptions of wealth, which excluded its highest forms, and thus restricted the scope of economic science by ruling out entire provinces of industry. Reinstate these departments of economic life, recognize the true wealth-producing function of such agents as the church and the school, and the extent and importance of the non-competitive division of political economy becomes apparent. We have hastily traced the boundaries of this division, with especial reference to the older portion of it. The free disbursal of products essential to the public welfare, has been secured by a departure from ordinary distributive methods. The ground of the radical difference between the two economic methods is a matter of both scientific and general interest, and we have found it in a teleologic principle in society, a quest for a wealth that, in quantity, quality, and distribution, shall conform to the requirements of enlightened reason. Within the limits which we have indicated, society has better attained its end by abandoning its usual competitive mode of action.

We have aimed, incidentally, to bring into view the

sovereignty of moral law in the economic practice of the world. If competition were supreme, it would be supremely immoral; if it existed otherwise than by sufferance, it would be a demon. Nothing could be wilder or fiercer than an unrestricted struggle of millions of men for gain, and nothing more irrational than to present such a struggle as a scientific ideal. If it be pruned of its greater enormities, as in actual life is done, if combinations restrict its field, and if arbitration and coöperation assume some of its functions, it still requires discernment to see the agency of moral law amid the abuses that remain. If, however, the sole end for which the process is tolerated is the suppression of greater and more general injustice, and if a superior power is ready to abolish it wherever it fails to fulfil this end, it may be classed, not as an ideal, but as an available means of approaching an ideal. In this view only are we secure from the blank confusion of supposing that the comprehensive field of economic life is alone outside of the controlling influence of morality. The insight that can detect providential design in the uglier forms of external nature, should detect it, also, in the repulsive phenomena of organized industry, in the "higgling of the market," the altercations of the civil law, and the ignoble scramble for personal profit.

As thus apprehended, there is no apotheosis of selfishness in the theory of political economy, and there is no necessarily corrupting effect from the practical outworking of its principles.   Recognizing the competitive struggle, wherever it survives, as the imperfect agent of moral law, a man may participate in it without taint. The bad effects of the contest he does not need to suffer; and to the lower levels, where the golden calf-worship is unhindered and blighting, he does not need to descend.   It is his privilege to live on the mountainous slope at the summit of which moral law reigns. He may buy, sell, and get gain, as well as give thanks and worship, with his eyes uplifted to the hills whence cometh his help.

CHAPTER XII.

THE daily bread of the world is the chief subject of political economy. If men were purely material, physical nourishment would suffice for them; but spiritual natures require spiritual nutriment. If what furnishes this nutriment were a purely immaterial thing, it would, as such, be removed from the domain of wealth, and thus from the field of economic science; but it is not so. It has, in fact, a material basis, and falls within the limits of the economist's studies; the students of this science have other than literal loaves to consider.

The consideration of forms of wealth which minister to spiritual wants is, indeed, necessary in the interest of religion. Certain modern religious problems need to be approached as well from the material as from the spiritual side; it is the economist who can, if he will, point out the chief danger which threatens the church. That which now concerns us is the fact that such a study is necessary in order to complete the science of political economy.

We have already noticed the wide range of application which current definitions of wealth must have if consistently adhered to. While wealth always has a material basis, that basis is not necessarily solid or durable. Vibrations of air may be shaped into artistic form by the violin or the voice, and become commodities as truly as the stone which is shaped by the sculptor's chisel. Such products as musical notes, perishable as they are, produce lasting effects on the mind, and are valuable accordingly in the market. Concert tickets convey a title to them, and these are not to be had without money. The delicate material commodities which diffuse themselves, for a time, through the concert hall, are essential to the spiritual effects which follow from their use; there could be none of the mental effects of music without the material undulations. As long as tremulous air thus holds within itself the power to impress the soul of man, it is subject for the economist; it is his business to investigate its laws as wealth. When these effects exist only as impressions on the mind, he may turn them over to the metaphysician; they are commodities no longer. Bread is a commodity only while on its way from the oven to the organ of digestion; after that it is subject for the physiologist; and that form of bread for the mind which we term music is, in like manner, a commodity only while *in transitu.*

Musical forms are not the only ones that can be impressed on vibrations of air. Marble may be chiselled into letters as well as images; and air vibrations may be shaped into forms of intelligence as well as into those of beauty. Spoken words may be commodities in the market, as well as musical notes. They are recognized as such; lecture tickets sometimes convey a title to them, and these are property, sold and paid for. A preacher's spoken word has, in like manner, its place on the inventory of social wealth; sermons, as delivered, are property. The hymn and the sermon are to be regarded as forms of nutriment for the soul, which are commodities while *in transitu* from their source to the organ of spiritual digestion.

Regarded in the prosaic light of economy, church edifices become places where spiritual nutriment is disbursed. Forms of wealth which minister to spiritual wants are here produced, distributed, exchanged, and consumed. Economic laws are general, and apply to higher as well as lower forms of wealth. Spiritually, we dine in commons, on the coöperative principle, once a week, with occasional lunches between whiles. The clergyman is a minister, in that he provides and distributes food. In former years the meals were prepared with Spartan simplicity; but of late they have been greatly elaborated. In spiritual as in physical meals, it is the appetizing element that is expensive; reduced to simple nutriment, a meal of either kind could be had very cheaply.

There is, then, a department of economic science which considers forms of material wealth which minister to spiritual wants. The relations of rich and poor are alike in the lower and the higher economic departments. The highest forms of wealth have their laws of distribution, and, in the course of social development, large classes are deprived of them. The laws of spiritual poor-relief are of importance to the economist.

The kind of spiritual poor-relief to be discussed here does not fall under the head of charity. Place a dozen men, each in his own boat, on the open sea, and start them for the nearest land. They are on an equality and completely independent. If any will not row, his destruction is on his own head. If any try to row and fail, it is the great law of charity, and that only, which constrains another to help him. If any venture to burden himself by towing a weaker brother to the shore, he is compelled to do so by no law legal or equitable, but the universal law of love.

But that is no picture of actual society. No man can paddle his own canoe as a member of that great social organism in which each individual labors, not for himself, but for the whole, and is dependent on the whole for employment and for pay. Independence is the law of isolation; interdependence is the law of society. Again and again, in actual history, society ceases to desire the product of a particular man's labor. The organic whole is in the position of employer to the millions who work, and it cannot always keep them busy; but it is not at liberty to starve

them. It may take away their comforts; but, if it
take their lives, it is murder. Civilization has placed
us all in one boat; by mutual help we are sailing the
homeward-bound ship of humanity. He who will not
help may be thrown overboard, possibly; but he who,
by force of circumstances, cannot, must be carried to
the end.

It is thus in the nature of the social organism that the
great principle of English law which asserts the ultimate
right of every man to a maintenance finds its philo-
sophical ground. That is an evil teaching which
ventures to question this principle, and it would fare ill
with a state which should attempt to follow such
teaching in practice. Such action would surrender to
the communists the championship of a great truth; it
would place society in the wrong, and revolutionists in
the right.

When a man who has had no hand in getting his
neighbor into trouble, lends his aid in getting him out,
that is charity. When an organized society relieves
suffering which the society as a whole has caused, that
is justice. Whatever part of the poor-tax goes to
relieve sufferings resulting from general social causes,
is paid, not given; the claim to it is as equitable as that
of any officer to his salary. We may assume as a
premise the principle asserted in the poor-law of Queen
Elizabeth, which established the right of every man,

not to be kept in idleness, indeed, but to be kept, while willing to work, from absolutely starving.

The higher nature may starve as well as the lower; and the duty of preventing such starvation has heretofore been made to rest mainly on spiritual grounds, and presented as a high order of charity. We place it on the ground of justice. The soul of man is not independent; the organic union of mankind includes mind as well as matter, and it is its nature, in every relation, to absorb and to subordinate the individual lives which are its molecules. He who is born into such a society is never independent in body or mind.

The healthy life of the soul of individual man is practically dependent on material aids; the higher life of the social organism is absolutely so dependent. Intercommunication is necessary to it. Sometimes by impressing forms of intelligence on insubstantial air, sometimes by printing them on more durable paper, an interchange of thought and feeling is established which unites the life of individuals into a single whole; it gives to society an organic soul.

That universal society, which, without any reference to particular sects, we term the church, controls the material aids to religious life. These aids are forms of wealth. The place of worship with its furnishings, the Bibles and books of song, much of the music, and most of the spoken words, are property, bought and paid for. Economic science stops at nothing in asserting its juris-

diction over what really belongs to it. It claims, even
to the farthest echo, the sound of the chimes that call
the worshippers together, when the paid organist rings
them. It ventures to claim the material instrument,
air vibrations still, by which the prayers of the assem-
bled multitude are held in unison and made to become
the prayer of an organic whole. There, however, its
audacious foot halts. The prayer itself is none of its
property; only the strictly material instrument that
expresses it. We have penetrated, in our scientific
temple, to the Gentiles' court, where buying and selling
are admissible; the inner sanctuary we may not enter.

Living not by literal bread alone, but by spiritual
impulses, foot-pounds of dynamic force which originate
beyond the sphere of matter, but diffuse themselves
through society by material means, man may starve
spiritually in consequence of material privation. Such
a famine is an economic fact, full of peril even to the
lower interests of society. The duty of averting it
has been recognized by civilized states, and a free disbursal of the means of intellectual and æsthetic culture
has partly accomplished this end. The distinctively
religious portion of this food for the mind has, by some
governments, been included in the public disbursal.
That our own government has surrendered this function
has been due, not to any undervaluation of the end to
be gained, but to an inability to gain it by state action.

The general conservation of moral energy is, indeed,

not altogether surrendered by the government; codes
of law are efficient educators. The religious department of popular education has been handed, as a sacred
trust, to voluntary organizations; and the duty rests on
them, in simple fidelity to the state, of continuing that
free disbursal of the highest products of human effort
which has always been essential to the public welfare,
and which is becoming doubly so, as the competitive
forms of industry diminish, and as the newer processes
of distribution increase.

The church has not been indifferent to this trust; it
is the great giver of modern times. Not a week passes
that it does not scatter its valuable products throughout the community. That which costs millions of
dollars is, in this way, offered without reserve to whoever will take it. The offer is not wholly rejected; in
the evening services of most churches, and in the morning services of many, there is seen a free disbursal of
the products on which the state is becoming more and
more dependent. Mere denunciation of the church for
delinquency in this direction is as mischievous as it is
unintelligent.

It is, of course, to be expected that, like the other
agencies which dispense rational wealth, the church
should procure what it disburses in the ordinary mercantile way. The cost of its products is governed by
ordinary laws. It must pay for buildings, furnishings
and books the prices which demand and supply deter-

mine. It must hire musicians and preachers at salaries which the tests of the market determine for their services. It is the disbursal of the products that should not be competitive. Here the principle of free giving to all who will accept should, in the interest of society, prevail, and the cost should be defrayed by non-mercantile methods. It may be that all who receive the products should contribute to the expense of creating them; but they should not buy them, and should certainly not buy the spiritual nutriment which the church offers in a vitiated form, or in combination with a base element attached to it for the purpose of making it saleable. This method of corrupting the merchandise of the church we shall examine.

The present industrial condition has come suddenly upon society; and it is partly for this reason that the interaction of economic and spiritual forces has only begun to receive attention. The trend of the old political economy was in the reverse direction; and we are but just becoming fully conscious that the industrial system depends absolutely on moral influences, and that these depend on material aids.

Even recent and valuable studies of the causes which have alienated workingmen from the church have failed to present clearly the distinctively economic element in the situation. This element is all that it is either desirable or legitimate to present here. Certain causes have vitiated the highest products of human effort, and have changed for the worse the mode of disbursing them. A low mercantile principle has, in an insidious way, acquired a degree of control over one department of church activity. Without the conscious acquiescence of the members of the church, and, of late, even against their wishes and efforts, the organization has become entangled in the meshes of the commercial system which environs it, and so ceased to be, to the extent which the public interest demands, the free disburser of rational wealth.

The causes and the effects of this half-unconscious breach of trust fall partly within the limits of economic study. There is difficulty inherent in the plan of maintaining different social classes at the same table, literal or spiritual. Under a *régime* of Spartan simplicity a community may be conceived of as dining literally in commons; but it is Spartan broth that they would get. Repeal the wise laws of Lycurgus against luxury, and the rich will soon have a table to themselves; and the manner in which this will come about illustrates what is occurring at our spiritual dining-table. With gold in his pocket, instead of corroded iron, a Spartan communist would want something better than barley soup. Under such circumstances the quality of the food would be likely to be improved. Under the influence of strong fraternal feeling the poor might remain for a time; but to pay their share would be burdensome, and to remain as beneficiaries would be irksome. They would gradually withdraw, and each withdrawal would facilitate the process of improving the quality of the meal and increasing its expense. The process would naturally continue until the wealthy should be left alone in the enjoyment of an elegant and costly entertainment.

Such a case is ideal; but it becomes actual when we consider not physical but spiritual living. The Puritan church of America lived in voluntary commons, in extreme simplicity. Its spiritual diet was nourishing, but the opposite of luxurious. Two centuries have seen the growth of differences of wealth, the adoption of a more luxurious spiritual table, and the withdrawal of a majority of the poor.

The introduction of costly elements into religious services might not have been a vitiating element in the disbursal of moral nutriment, had the needed revenue come from the public treasury. It appears not to have that effect in the Roman Catholic church of European countries. The revenue system of the American Protestant church is the peculiar product of a mercantile age. It is not too much to say that this organization has, in comparative unconsciousness, developed the most unworthy form of mercantilism which the old economic *régime* has brought into existence. The competitive system, in its latter days, has laid an evil hand upon the activities of the church.

We noticed, in an early chapter of this book, the

dominant influence of fashion in the production and sale of many utilities. The product which has a caste-making power becomes thereby an object of intense desire. The costliest products of nature and art command their price because they act as badges of social station. Give to the homeliest article of common necessity a supplementary power to mark its possessor as a superior atom in the social organism, and he will pay a high price for it. The garment that is cut according to the latest mode appeals to a simple natural want and to personal vanity at the same time. The jewel that is to-day in vogue satisfies an æsthetic want which counts as one, and an ambitious craving which counts as ten, in the determining of its market value. Each of these products is a composite of rational utility and vanity; and each depends on the latter element for its costliness.

The church makes, for financial reasons, a similar combination; and the disastrous feature of the process is that the baser and costlier element here vitiates the better one. The church does not literally sell the gospel; it practically gives it away, and gets a revenue from the base tinsel which it combines with it. It rents pews, and so grades them as to appeal to the same subtle weakness of human nature which gives a high market value to everything which has a caste-making power. He who pays for one pew ten times the price that would secure another differently located pays little or nothing for spiritual nutriment; he pays something for comfort, and much for the gratification of that subtle ambition which everywhere craves the high places in the social gradation. The proceeding draws lines of caste, in indefinite number, throughout the audience-room, and invokes, for the purpose of raising a revenue, a spirit which is well known to be fatal not only to the success of the spiritual work for which the church was founded, but also to the success of the work which the state demands of it in the new industrial era.

If a new and higher type of industrial organization shall develop from the present chaotic condition, it will be one that will have, as its distinctive principle, fraternity among men. It will harmonize warring elements, and enable humanity to live by accepting, as a great family, the bounty of nature, working in harmony and dividing the fruits of labor in peace. As the fountain-head of the chief moral and spiritual influence, the church should be the great unifier, the principal author of that fraternal spirit on which higher industrial development depends. It is, in fact, the promoter of class antagonism; by its method of gaining a revenue it is widening the gulf that needs to be closed.

A church that openly appeals to the caste spirit destroys its power to assimilate the multitude for whose welfare it exists, loses its vitalizing principle, and becomes a lump which, though in itself it were manna,

will not leaven a measure of meal, though it lie hidden
in it forever. Wiser than the children of light are the
members of the friendly societies, secret orders, and
trades unions which modern economic tendencies have
developed. Whatever of moral nutriment they disburse they scatter among their members on a demo-
cratic principle. The church must do likewise or
surrender its moral leadership. It must fight the
caste-making tendency as it would the Spirit of Dark-
ness, and not foster it, Demas-like, for the revenue
which it offers.

Entering on a course that is as full of peril as it is of
promise, society demands that every moral agency shall
be in the fullest working order. Least of all can it
dispense with the work that addresses itself directly to
the personal character of individual men. Everywhere
we hear the appeal to the church, as the agent that
can most efficiently aid in the economic redemption of
humanity. There can be no retreat in the general
course of moral progress upon which the world has
lately entered ; and institutions as well as men are to
be sifted by it. "On earth peace ; " such is the fruit
by which we are to know a church that is true to the
mission for which it was founded. Fraternity is the
result and the test of true Christianity working through
sound economic forms. This test, if intelligently applied, will be found to condemn, not the spirit of the
church, but its outward methods. That the organiza-

tion which now broadens the gulf between social classes may become the chief agent in closing it, there is needed, not the miracle of a totally new spirit among its members, but the adoption of outward forms less mercantile than those now prevalent, and more in harmony with the new economic era.

It is sometimes said that men must be actuated in all their dealings by Christian love, if the labor question is ever to be settled. This is demanding a transformation of human nature, and is equivalent to abandoning the hope of securing a favorable issue of the contests now in progress by means of forces at present available. Humanity is approaching the Christian ideal surely and not always slowly; it will be nearer to it next year than it is now, and it will doubtless be appreciably nearer to it when the next generation is upon the field of action. More generations must pass than any one can estimate before the ideal will be fully attained; and in the meanwhile the social conflict is upon us. Have we nothing to oppose to the brute forces that, in a night, as it were, have sprung into full activity, except the margin of moral improvement which an interval of waiting and working may secure?

It is the duty of the economist to study social forces as they are, or at least as they will be in the near future. Influences which ought now to exist, and which will exist in a millennial age, are not material for present economic calculation. The characteristic of

the changes in actual progress in the business world is
the liberation of moral energy; an existing force has
been unfettered by the industrial revolution. The competitive system in its degenerate form held under repres-
sion a limitless moral power which the better system
now developing is already beginning to call into action.
The church is the natural conservator of this force, not
only within the limits of its membership, but in society
at large. In many ways it diffuses the spiritual impulses that are communicated to it; and while this work
still has, as its chief end, the moulding of character itself, it has, as a secondary end, the improvement of the
economic relations of men. The church wields a primary force in the new economic system, and is, to that
extent, an arbiter of men's earthly fortunes. In a literal sense its field is the world; and while it may
hasten the advent of earthly peace by gathering men
more rapidly into its spiritual fold, it may also hasten
the spiritual work by promoting outward harmony. To
a certain extent the higher service waits on the lower,
and for the sake of every interest entrusted to its keep-
ing the church is called upon to use the economic
power entrusted to it.

*9 7 8 3 3 3 7 0 7 3 5 5 8 *